Exquisite Jesus

Keith Jackson

Onwards and Upwards Publishers

3 Radfords Turf
Cranbrook
Exeter
EX5 7DX

www.onwardsandupwards.org

Printed in the UK.

ISBN: 978-1-911086-38-3
Typeface: Sabon LT
Graphic design: LM Graphic Design

Endorsements

This is a book about Jesus. Keith Jackson comes with fresh eyes to the most compelling person in all of history and asks some of the Big Questions about Jesus: who He is, why He came and what His life, death and message have to do with us today.

In a world where so much information is available instantly, Keith goes deep and lingers long in the amazing life and ministry of Jesus as revealed in the Bible.

Keith's aim is not just to inform but to present the person of Jesus in a way that draws the reader into real relationship with Him. He writes with wisdom, insight and great passion in order that we might not simply know about Jesus but know Him for ourselves.

Chris Cartwright
General Superintendent of the Elim Pentecostal Churches

In a challenging, unique and inspiring way, Keith Jackson helps us to look again at the person of Jesus. Using personal stories and re-telling of biblical texts he has written a book that, if you grasp its message, will change your life.

I am proud to call Keith my pastor and friend. I have benefitted from many of his talks. He and Barbie are the real deal and their love for Jesus is contagious. Grab yourself a copy and read about the God who moved into our neighbourhood and changed everything.

Patrick Regan OBE
Founder & CEO of XLP

The three biggest questions in the universe are "Who is God?" "Why am I here?" and "Where am I in relation to God?" In this lucid and readable book, laced with personal anecdote, Keith Jackson draws from Scripture and long pastoral experience to address ... these vital issues.

John Glass
Chair of the Evangelical Alliance and
Former General Superintendent of the Elim Pentecostal Churches

About the Author

When Keith met God, everything changed. Having grown up in a home of broken dreams, spiritualism and divorce, he found himself on a new path with a new hope. Hearing the call of God soon after, he began to aim his life in service of the King.

With many years of pastoral and church leadership experience, Keith's practical wisdom unfolds through everything he does. Privileged to serve as the Lead Pastor of Life Church, a thriving Elim Pentecostal Church in Chelmsford, he seeks to honour God in everything he does.

Keith is a dynamic leader and a speaker renowned for his articulate and humorous communication style. He is passionate about bringing people into a deeper relationship with Christ through practically applying the Word of God to daily life.

Keith has lived in South Africa, the Isle of Man and England. He is married to Barbie and they reside in Essex, South East England.

For

Matt and Rio,
Ben and Emma,
Sam and Susanna.

He loves you passionately,
stubbornly, eternally.

Contents

Acknowledgements

None of what I do is possible without the amazing support of Barbie, my longsuffering, faithful and extraordinary wife. People have asked where I found the time to write a book whilst leading a large, vibrant church. The truth is, Barbie sacrificed more than I did as I spent much of our holidays and my weekly day off writing. She probably enjoyed the peace and quiet, supporting the project and doing the initial proofreading. She and Sam, our youngest son, also enjoyed debating some of the more theologically challenging parts.

Thanks, too, go to my fellow pastors at Life Church during this season, Phil "Rocky" Hannam and James "J.R." Richardson, as we discussed various ideas and doctrinal foundations. Always an inspiration, they've been amazing! Thank you also to our elders who have continually asked how things are going and have awaited their copies of this book with great patience!

I am a truly blessed man to have had so many great pastors, friends and mentors over the years. I am truly grateful for the love and friendship of John Harrison, Billy Fenning, Jonathan Stanfield, Mike Alcock, Dave Redbond, Dave Campbell and John Glass.

Luke Jeffery and the team at O&U, thanks for having faith in a new kid on the publishing block!

Finally, although He is the First and Last in all things, thank you Jesus. Your love for a bloke like me constantly astounds me. I owe you a debt that I can never pay, and look forward to the next chapter as the pages of the book of my life that you are authoring continue to be written.

Prologue

I have been following Jesus since 1980. In fact, I have walked with Him longer than I lived without Him. I have found in those years that He has been more than a Saviour and more than a Lord. He has been my friend. My keeper. My one and truly trusted confidant. He has helped me out of messes that I seem to get myself into. He has guided me in my life and sent me on a course of service and adventure that I could never have fully anticipated at the beginning. The exciting thing for me is that it is not over yet (I hope).

When I became a Christian God showed me several things He wanted to use my life for; at least, gave me an inkling of them. Some of these have come to pass. Others have not – yet. One of the 'not yet' things was to author books. Over the years I have had numerous ideas, half-heartedly started with something and stopped. It just never seemed to be the right time in His plan, nor my ever increasingly busy schedule, to sit and write. I know of some who started writing the moment they were saved. I know of others who have written several books and have been Christians a short time.

I simply did not want to write until I felt the smile of Father God for it. The moment of inspiration, if it is that, came when I was researching for an apologetics module in our church's Bible School. I was re-reading John Stott's classic, *Issues Facing Christians Today.* In it he wrote:

> *We need to see him in his paradoxical fullness – his sufferings and glory, his servanthood and lordship, his lowly incarnation and cosmic reign.*[1]

Pop! Lightbulb moment. *Write about Jesus! Write about His paradoxical greatness yet vulnerability.* I then turned to my own denominational movement's statement of faith, our Foundational Truths, and read again these words:

---

1 John Stott, *Issues Facing Christians Today,* (Zondervan, Grand Rapids, 2006, 4th Ed.), p54.

> *The Saviour: We believe in the true and proper deity of our Lord Jesus Christ, in His virgin birth, in His real and complete humanity, in His sinless life, in His authoritative teaching, in His substitutionary and atoning sacrifice through His blood shed, in His bodily resurrection, in His ascension to the right hand of the Father, in His heavenly intercession and His second advent to receive His Church.*

There's a lot in there and some of it to many people is gobbledygook. This is not a theological textbook. There are enough of those around. This is a book that looks at Jesus' apparent contradictions within Himself:

- How can He be God yet die on a cross?
- Did the virgin birth really happen?
- Does He heal?
- Why do some people follow Him and some not?

Yes, it's a book that tries to answer some questions. It is also a book that as I have written it, I have found my love for Jesus growing even more. I hope that as you read through these pages, you too will fall in love with Him again, or maybe even meet Him for the first time. I also include some personal anecdotes and some re-telling of the biblical texts, so you can discover afresh the relevance of Jesus to your life.

Why 'exquisite'? As an adjective, 'exquisite' tries to portray the meaning that something, or someone, is beautiful, lovely, superb, valuable, delicate, priceless, beyond description and more. I use it to try and capture the opposites of who Jesus is: fully human, fully God, combined into one. I hope and pray as you read through the following pages that the exquisiteness of Jesus becomes real to you.

PART ONE

His Image

He is the image of the invisible
God, the firstborn over all creation.

Colossians 1:15

CHAPTER ONE

Family Likeness

What does God look like?

He looks like Jesus. More accurately, Jesus looks like Him.

What does Jesus look like?

Over the years artists have painted Christ in their own image. He is sometimes portrayed as blonde, with blue piercing eyes, a slightly tanned complexion and a half smile reassuringly gazing from the canvas. This is a Western image of Christ. In African nations He is often depicted as of African heritage. His eyes are always loving and the half smile is usually there. In art throughout the centuries the pattern repeats across cultural divides and geographic boundaries. Latterly people have depicted Jesus artistically as a rebel; a guerrilla fighter; a perfectly toothed, whiter-than-white, grinning, smiling Jesus; as gay; or as angry.

All of these, like all other depictions, are in some measure to make Jesus like us. We want Him in our image. He's not.

He is gloriously God's image.

There is a stunning lack of a physical description of Jesus' looks in the New Testament. We are told of His qualities. Perhaps that's the point. There can be no racial divide when it comes to Christ. He is the Saviour of the whole world, not just your part of it.

The glory of God is in Christ. There is a reclamation of the image of God in Christ's humanity. The mystery of His divinity is that He is fully man, fully God. His humanity carried the image of God as all humanity does. Before time, before the earth or the universe existed, the Godhead was. Not created. Not imagined by anyone. Not thought of. Pre-existent. Within this perfect union of three-yet-one came the will for the existence of the universe. From God's will came the desire for a creature so unique, so empowered with potential, that this organic form would carry the image of God.

> *Then God said, "Let us make man in our image, in our likeness, and let them rule over the fish of the sea and the birds of the air, over the livestock, over all the earth, and over all the creatures that move along the ground." So God created man in his own image, in the image of God he created him; male and female he created them.*[2]

---

2 Genesis 1:26-27.

Chapter Two

In His Image

In the heart of God was a desire for a creature that was in His image. He created humanity, you and me, with that in mind. Does this mean that God physically looks like you and me? Two eyes, a nose, a mouth, ears, hands, feet and flesh and bone? The Bible is replete with anthropomorphisms, where God is described as having human characteristics; He is described as having hands, feet and eyes and more.[3] That does not mean He physically has these; they are attempts to describe the indescribable.

Whilst Jesus most commonly refers to God as Father throughout His ministry, describing their overriding relationship, he is also clear that God is Spirit.[4] He is telling you that Father God is not like you. *You* are created in *His* image. *You* are meant to be like *Him.*

God breathed life into Adam, the first man, setting him apart from creation.

> *...the Lord God formed the man from the dust of the ground and breathed into his nostrils the breath of life, and the man became a living being.*[5]

This meant that Adam and the rest of humankind that followed were significantly different to the rest of creation, possessing a spirit,

---

3 Ecclesiastes 9:1.
4 John 4:24.
5 Genesis 2:7.

an eternal element to their being that is placed there by God Himself. Humanity is set apart from the rest of the animals inhabiting the earth. Why? Because within the heart of the Godhead was a desire to create a creature so wonderful, so capable of greatness and dominion, so intrinsically beautiful that God could breathe His very life into it.

Genetics do not separate humans that much from the rest of the living creatures. God formed humankind from the earth He had already created. It is no wonder that evolutionists berate the idea of a Creator when the physical matter that is shared is so similar. It has been said that people share ninety-eight percent of their genes with a common rat. Put like this, it casts to doubt that there is a design, a purpose and a loving God behind it all. Although I am no scientist I do understand that the sequence in which DNA is laid down has a dramatic effect on what subsequently develops. Many headlines about the similarities between humans and other mammals are based upon the selection of a very few parallels between the two rather than the vast differences between species.[6] Although pointing to something that is true, this approach is biased. One of my daughters-in-law is from Spain, but her main home language is Catalan as she is from the North East of the country. To the untrained ear, Spanish and Catalan sound the same, and at times use the same words, but they are very different languages. In the same way, to say a human is the same as a rat is to deny the differences that clearly exist! A woman probably won't want to marry a rat, although she might have dated a few! The intentionality of the Grand Designer cannot be easily dismissed.

Jesus is the image of the invisible God. He claimed that if someone had seen Him they had seen the Father.[7] This is a massive claim. He is not stating that God is *like* Him but that *He is God too.* It's a claim of divinity. When asked by His disciples to show them Father, for that would be enough for them, they were relating the ultimate ideal for the Jewish traditions: to have God revealed to them. That would be sufficient, substantial and carry them through life. Jesus said they had seen Father by seeing, knowing and being with

---

6 Jeffrey P. Tomkins, *Common DNA Sequences: Evidence of Evolution or Efficient Design?* http://www.icr.org/article/common-dna-sequences-evidence-evolution, accessed on 15/06/16.

7 John 14:9.

Him. How could He say this? He understood that what they asked for is what Paul would write about later in Colossians. Jesus is the image of Father God.

A few verses later Paul writes:

For God was pleased to have all his fullness dwell in him.[8]

The image of true humanity had to be reclaimed and restored. The moment sin entered the hearts of Adam and Eve, a lament rang out across the creation. The whole of the universe was now in a perpetual state of decay and at war with itself. Humanity began to display inhumane acts. They began to forget about their Creator and in each subsequent generation moved farther and farther away from the image that they were created in, one small step at a time. That image had become tarnished, forgotten, maligned and ultimately thought of as a myth, a man-made story to give false hope. Humanism replaced humanity. Life became disposable. Eventually, inevitably, science became the new god, claiming its theories delivered all the answers, without properly understanding the question, *why are we here?*

The image had to be restored. Only one could do that. God had to come incarnate. He would have to walk the earth He created and breathe the air He designed. He would have to gaze upon the stars in the sky from humanity's perspective, watch sunrises and sunsets in distant horizons. He would have to live within the Creation that pointed to His own existence and glory. He would have to become a man.

A perfect sinless man. A man who would die for sin. A man who would restore the image once again.

---

8 Colossians 1:19.

CHAPTER THREE

Looking Good

We are image-driven in the Western world. It's so ingrained within us that we do not even notice that it is happening. You may be reading this and think, "No, I'm not! Surely, image is the plague of the younger generation!"

Let me ask you a question to see if there may be some truth to this. In your home, do you have a mirror in the hallway so you can quickly check how you look before leaving the house? Don't panic – we have one in our home too! In fact, it is very hard in our culture not to see reflections of ourselves in shop windows and public places throughout our day. For most people, when this happens, it is almost impossible to ignore the reflection and keep on walking.

We are all affected by a quest for the right image. The image we project is the story we are telling the world about ourselves. It may be a story of wealth, success, out-of-date fashion, low income, fitness or overeating. Other people judge our image. We size each other up in a few seconds of meeting or seeing someone in the street. We form opinions, pigeonholing people with a glance.

This happens in church too. My wife Barbie grew up in church. She comes from a Christian home and gave her life to Jesus at about four years old. She was not allowed to wear jeans, or even slacks, to church. It had to be a dress. The rest of the week this rule didn't apply, but when it was time for church on Sunday, or even the youth group on a Friday, out would come the dress. Years later she still asks me when we are getting ready for church if it would be alright for her to wear trousers.

I did not grow up in church. My story could not be more different from my wife's. I wear jeans to preach in or smart slacks depending on my mood in the morning. Our church knows when there is a wedding or a funeral by what I am wearing! I have my image hang-ups too; they are just not the same my wife's.

Years later Barbie asked her mother about the wear-a-dress-to-church thing when we were going to church with her and her mother was wearing slacks. Her mother thought about it and said, "I don't think any of us knew why we did it; we just knew that's what you did." Her mother was not a bad person. In fact, she was probably one of the saintliest people I ever met.

There are social conventions in the church, image concerns. I come across it all the time. I have been in churches that seem to value scruffiness and designer stubble, a look that says, "We came today with no time to shower, get ready, but God looks at the heart, right?" It's a church culture that prides itself on a lack of image, breaking with conventions.

I've also been to a church that seemed to value the power of the comb-over to hold back male pattern baldness. I kid you not! My wife and I were visiting and sat on the balcony. We looked across the congregation and there, amongst the hats and traditional wear, were about nine or so men with increasingly elaborate comb-overs. These varied from the straight, left-to-right, slicked-down variety to the three-way layered beehives held in place with lashings of hairspray. When we left the church it was, sadly, a windy day, and all these faithful brothers ended up trying to hold their creations in place as the wind did its worst! It is still an image culture at work. More accurately it is a homogenous culture at work. People like to hang out with people like themselves. Within a few years this becomes the culture of the church, a tradition.

The mistake is in thinking that 'image' is to do with the physical. It isn't. 1 Peter 3:3 says:

> *Your beauty should not come from outward adornment, such as braided hair and the wearing of gold jewellery and fine clothes...*

This verse is speaking to women of the day, but the point being made here is that the outward image does not matter if the inward is corrupt. What is on the inside will ultimately show up on the outside.

CHAPTER FOUR

What Do You Look For?

Samuel had a dilemma. He'd travelled to the home of Jesse to anoint the new King even though the former King, Saul, was alive. (God had rejected Saul.) Samuel saw Eliab, the oldest, and thought, "Job done! This guy's perfect!" He was wrong. The world is full of Eliabs who look good but have little substance. What was needed was someone different. Someone with character. A worshipper of God. Someone of faith. Someone whom God would eventually say was a man after His own heart.

Gently the Father spoke into the heart of Samuel:

> *"Do not consider his appearance or his height, for I have rejected him. The Lord does not look at the things man looks at. Man looks at the outward appearance, but the Lord looks at the heart."*[9]

Eliab reminded Samuel of Saul: tall, good-looking, square-jawed, an impressive specimen. God was looking at the heart.

Seven brothers passed by Samuel's eye that day. Nothing from God. No nudge, no "thus saith The Lord". Silence from heaven. It behoves us to wait longer and not be impetuous if we are facing life-changing decisions.

Samuel asked a question. Having seen seven sons and still not heard from God he could have packed up the sacrifice he had brought

---

[9] 1 Samuel 16:7.

and moved on. He didn't. It was too important. "Have you got any more sons?" To our ears this sounds a little odd. Surely seven sons are enough for anyone! Maybe Samuel had a hunch that someone was out working somewhere if these seven had all lined up in front of him.

There *was* another son: the youngest, who was out tending sheep. In other words, he was not that important. Shepherding was dangerous work and involved putting yourself between predators and the flock. It was also boring work with many hours spent in solitude. It was not the type of work you would send the firstborn son to do. He was important. He would get the birthright. Apparently it wasn't work that the other six sons would do either. They had probably all done it at some point but when a new child was born the older brother would be counting the days for him to be old enough to go shepherding on his own.

What others saw as unimportant God saw as training. In solitude David learnt to worship God and play the harp. In danger David learnt to fight off bears and lions with a sling. He came to realise that the strength of men fails but that God is all sufficient, all powerful and not to be messed with. Was it not David who answered the challenge of Goliath, who was coming against The Lord of Hosts?[10] In the wilderness looking after sheep David came to realise that image was formed in the heart based on what God said about him, not what others thought about him.

---

[10] 1 Samuel 17.

CHAPTER FIVE

As Secure as Jesus

Jesus is the image of the unseen God. To know what that image looks like we need to begin to understand that Jesus' security came from what God said about Him.

He could see the crowds at the Jordan and hear the distant voice of his cousin[11] carrying across the expanse, rising to a crescendo. "I baptise you with water for repentance. But after me will come one who is more powerful than I, whose sandals I am not fit to carry. He will baptise you with the Holy Spirit and with fire. His winnowing fork is in his hand, and he will clear his threshing floor, gathering his wheat into the barn and burning up the chaff with unquenchable fire."[12]

Perhaps Jesus smiled as He heard the words, John preaching repentance and judgment in one breath. Didn't he know that Jesus had come to save the world, not condemn it? In God's heart there is a long pause between salvation and the judgment to come.

Pushing His way through the throng their eyes met.

John hesitates. He knows why Jesus is there... but surely not! How can this be? As Jesus enters the Jordan, John cries out, "I need to be baptised by you, and do you come to me?"[13]

Jesus smiled. Like all prophets John saw much but not all things.

---

11 Matthew 3:11-16.

12 verses 11-12.

13 verse 14b.

Jesus replied, "Let it be so now; it is proper for us to do this to fulfil all righteousness."

Then John consented. Jesus had to fulfil all righteousness. Being baptised as a man for Him was not a baptism of repentance. It fulfilled something required of Him by God. A fulfilment of righteousness. An acknowledgement that whilst divine, He was fully human too, and that humanity was weak and subject to temptation. His baptism was an acknowledgement that if this salvation plan was to work, He was going to have to fully depend on God as a man. It was a consecration.

Thunder! The thunderous voice of God rings out across the galaxy. "THIS IS MY SON, WHOM I LOVE; WITH HIM I AM WELL PLEASED." The clouds part and the Holy Spirit descends like a dove.[14] For the first time in thirty years the Trinity are reunited, ever so briefly, but that moment thrills heaven, and Hades trembles.

Three Promises for Jesus

God says three things about Jesus for those who could understand what was happening. These three things would sustain Jesus too.

Firstly, "You are my Son." We know that Jesus' default name for God in prayer is Father. Father's favourite name for Jesus in these intimate moments is Son. Jesus, as a result of being God incarnate, has stepped into a realm to be enjoyed by Christians ever since: to be a child of God. Jesus is God's only begotten son. There also had to be the declaration from God of this paternity.

We are all created in the image of God. That image is tarnished. For the image to display the family likeness of the Father there has to be a claiming back of the family name. Jesus had committed no sin, never did. Humanity had. Jesus had to become what the writer of Corinthians called the 'second Adam' – and to do this He had to be acknowledged as the 'first child'.[15]

"I love Him," is the second thing God says to and about Jesus. This is no superfluous use of the phrase that we have in our society

---

14 Note: The Bible doesn't say that the Spirit *was* a dove, but *like* a dove, meaning that He is gentle, soothing and peaceful. Doves will never alight on a corpse or rotting flesh, but only that which is alive.

15 1 Corinthians 15:20-22.

today. It is not change of status on social media with little hearts next to it. This is a dramatic statement. A parent's love for their child knows no limits. It is effervescent and passionate. It does not wilt, nor die, nor lose its fervour. In Father God's case it is a continuum that echoes throughout the eons and seeks to touch the heart of every man, woman and child who has lived or ever will live. For Jesus this is a powerful infusion of love that He will display to others innumerable times over the next three-and-a-half years and, ultimately, that love will keep Him through the curse of the cross.

Thirdly, "I am well pleased with you!" This is a Father's blessing. The Old Testament gives us several occurrences of when the Father's blessing was passed to the firstborn and subsequent children. Jacob gave a blessing to all of his sons, as his father had done, although he stole his brother Esau's birthright.[16] The blessing was not just a sign that the father was about to die, although this is normally given when there are obvious signs of fragility and decay, but it was also a sign of the pleasure a father took in a son.

Father God is making it perfectly clear to Jesus and the listeners that He has blessed Jesus. He doesn't just say, "I am pleased," but, "I am *well* pleased." There is an overuse of the word 'well' in parts of the east of London and into the county of Essex in England. When something is good or to be commended or to be emphasised as wrong, many will add 'well' as a form of exclamatory prefix. That was "well good" or "well bad". This phrase in the Gospels is not an indication that God is from Essex! It does carry an emphasis we should not miss.

It is a statement that God is emphatic in His pleasure, He is pleased to be pleased with Jesus.

The image was now being restored and acknowledged in the heavens. The second Adam was in place.

Three Promises for You

The three statements that Father spoke over Jesus have dynamic relevance for you today. Everyone is created in the image of God and therefore has an intrinsic value. No one can walk in that image untarnished, as Adam and Eve first did, in their own self-worth or

---

16 Genesis 49:1-28 cf. Hebrews 11:20-21; Genesis 25:29-34.

purity. Sin makes sure of this. Yet God desires to speak the three statements He spoke to Jesus to your heart too because Jesus, through His sacrifice, has made it possible.

The death of Jesus that brings forgiveness of sins needs to be seen from the viewpoint of, *who is granting the forgiveness?* Jesus gives a clue on the cross:

> *"Father, forgive them, for they do not know what they are doing."*[17]

Father God is the one who forgives. The cross makes it possible for you to hear these three things today:

- You are God's child.
- You are loved.
- Father takes pleasure in you.

Jesus made a way for your adoption. There are three ways to become a member of a family: by birth; by adoption; by marriage. I have experienced all three. Obviously I was born into a family. Shortly afterwards my biological parents divorced and a relatively short time later my mother remarried. I was then adopted by my step-father. When this occurred all parental responsibilities and legal requirements of my biological father were voided, as though they had never existed. In 1988 I married and became part of my wife's family.

The Bible has the same analogies to describe becoming part of God's family: being born again, being adopted and being part of the Bride.[18]

Jesus is the "one and only Son", meaning a physical union has taken place.[19] This fact, declared from the heavens, opened up the way for you to be born again. You are adopted. That means all legal rights of your previous life have now been made null and void.

Over the years I have known some families who cannot have children and some of these choose to adopt. It's an emotional process and I admire these new parents greatly. Sometimes, when there has been an adoption, the mother will conceive naturally. Not always,

---

17 Luke 23:34.

18 John 3:3; Ephesians 1:5; Revelation 22:17.

19 John 3:16.

just sometimes. With God it was the opposite. He fathers Jesus and then adopts you.

CHAPTER SIX

More than Rescued!

An adopter is different to a rescuer.

A *rescuer* can be described as a saviour. Imagine you are walking beside a river and you see a person fall in. You see they are in danger of drowning and being swept away by the current. Grabbing a nearby rope, you throw an end to the person struggling in the water. They grab it and you use all your strength to pull them to the river bank. His relief is overwhelming. You hug and make sure that he gets home. He is safe. You are a hero. Moving forward in life, you may exchange Christmas cards, the odd pleasantry as you pass in the street, and if he outlives you he might come and say a few words at your funeral. That's it. There is no responsibility placed upon a rescuer to do more. Job done.

A *redeemer* is a slightly different picture in the Bible. Jesus is described as your Redeemer. He is compared often with Boaz in the book of Ruth.[20] A redeemer is one who pays a price to purchase another out of slavery or destitution. The Bible says you have been purchased by your Redeemer. This was a costly thing. In the biblical tradition you now no longer belonged to someone else or even yourself, you belonged to the one who had paid the price.

A good redeemer will be righteous. A bad redeemer may enforce you into a new kind of slavery that is worse than the one you have been delivered from. Jesus is obviously the perfect Redeemer. He sets

---

[20] Ruth 2:20.

you free.[21] In essence though, when an earthly redeemer has set you free, you now enjoy free choice on how to live. The Bible implores you to recognise this new relationship – you have been bought at a price and are no longer your own – but there is no denying you have a free will. Essentially, too, a redeemer's role is over once the slavery has ended. You are free.

The relationship between the redeemer and the slave is stronger than the relationship between the rescuer and the rescued. This is because those needing rescue, although living through a trauma, can re-establish their lives fairly quickly compared to those who have experienced the extended trauma of slavery. Ultimately, though, redeemers will desire to take a hands-off approach as they help people rebuild their lives. There is always a deep friendship but there is also an end point to the responsibility of the modern day redeemer.

An *adopter* is different to a rescuer and a redeemer. The qualities of the rescuer and redeemer can be seen in the adopter. The adopter rescues. They save those in distress and give an opportunity for life to continue. The adopter redeems. They pay a higher price than a rescuer. They help rehabilitate a child who may have experienced separation, trauma or, sadly, abuse at the hands of others. Unlike the rescuer and the redeemer, however, an adopter makes the rescued and the redeemed part of the family. The adopter calls the child "Son" or "Daughter". They give them the family name. All legal rights that were in place before are now voided. The legal status of the child changes. They now have a new life, a home, a family and, ultimately, an inheritance.[22]

Your exquisite Jesus is your Rescuer, your Saviour. He has thrown you the lifeline to grab hold of and be pulled out of your mess to the safety of the river bank. Jesus is your Redeemer. He has paid the price for your sin and has taken the punishment for you. He has enabled you to be rehabilitated and build a new life, a life that is abundant and full.[23] He has done more than this though. He has

---

21 Luke 4:18.

22 The comparisons between rescuer, adopter and redeemer were inspired by a short talk by Krish Kandiah, at The Bridge, Elim International Conference Centre, Malvern, February 2015.

23 John 10:10.

made a way for you to be adopted by Father God.[24] This means you are now a joint heir with Jesus. You share in His rewards. You share too in His sufferings.[25] Legally everything has changed. You have moved from a kingdom ruled by darkness to the Kingdom of light.[26] We carry the family name: Christian; follower of Christ or Christ-like one.

Jesus made a way for the lavish love of God to be enjoyed. Parents love their children. It is natural. Something changes within the heart of a man when he holds his baby for the first time. There is an overwhelming desire to protect and provide for the new life in his arms. My wife and I have been blessed to have three sons. All of them are exceptional, fine young men. When we were expecting our second child my wife confided in me that she was nervous about the impending arrival. When I asked why she replied, "I'm not sure that my heart is big enough to love two." I tried to be reassuring but, to be honest, was lost for words and simply hugged her. Things like this a man stashes away for the future in case there are problems ahead. The birth came and went reasonably well although our son didn't breathe for the first minute. This was a little traumatic but when he filled the room with his cries it was one of the most joyful sounds we had ever heard. Sometime later I reminded my wife of our earlier conversation. Her reply taught me a lesson. "Oh, that," she said. "My heart just got bigger!"

If you are a mother of children you will instantly understand what my wife meant. I am not sure I can prove how big God's heart and His capacity for loving you is. I am not sure if His heart grows each time a person becomes His child. I am not sure if His heart has a defined boundary, a set limit, on how many people He can love. I figure the clue is in John 3:16; He has a capacity to love the *whole world* – those that were then, those that are now, and those that will be to come. I do know this: His heart has room for *you!* That love is a stubborn and forceful love that compels the whole of Creation to long for the full number of believers to be accounted for.[27]

---

24 Romans 8:15.
25 Romans 8:17.
26 Ephesians 5:8.
27 Romans 8:18-25.

You are not the exception that proves the rule. God loves you. Lavishly. He loves you with an everlasting love.[28] Jesus made a way for God to show you His pleasure. Father's desire is to bless you. That does not mean that God is only concerned with your happiness. I hear parents all the time who say that their only wish for their children is that they are happy. How do those same parents cope when their children do things under the banner of happiness that are patently destructive? That kind of happiness is narcissistic. The truth is, no parent simply wants happiness for their children. They want their children to have happiness but not at all costs for they know true happiness is not found from within.

When God shows you His good pleasure He is saying, "This is my beloved child in whom I am well pleased!" He begins to bless you in spite of what is happening around you. Jesus did not say that we would always be happy or that we would have a smooth ride as Christians:

> *"I have told you these things, so that in me you may have peace. In this world you will have trouble."*[29]

Take note that He promises you peace in Him. He also tells you that in this world, in this chronological timeframe in which you live, this segment of eternity, that you will have trouble as His follower. As Christians we often ignore this cautionary phrase, shunning the idea of difficulties. When I became a Christian, life around me fell apart. Shortly after, my mother left home to live with her boyfriend, returning on weekends to ensure that there was at least food at home for my brother and me. During this period, we were burgled several times, the last of which resulted in arson and the destruction of everything we had. Added to this, I was mercilessly bullied at school and found myself physically and emotionally victimised to the point where I skipped a portion of my high school education. These were tough years for my brother and me. I did not feel especially blessed.

Jesus went on to say:

> *"But take heart! I have overcome the world."*[30]

---

[28] Psalm 103:17; Jeremiah 31:3.
[29] John 16:33a.
[30] John 16:33.

Now, that is a word of hope! It is a promise of provision and blessing. No matter what comes your way, Father has made a way for His pleasure to be displayed in spite of it. His blessings may be tangible, material or emotional. They may be intangible too. Sometimes it can be hard to see the hand of God at work in your life in a given instance. Sometimes the fingerprint of God is difficult to see. Occasionally He appears to wear gloves. Resonant always, He still cries out from heaven that you are His. His pleasure. He is well pleased with you!

The image of God is restored in Jesus as God's Son. That image is shown in you as His adopted child. It is not displayed through a physical appearance, but normally through the character and the fruit of someone's life. The fruit of the Spirit found in Galatians give you an overview of what the image of God is like: loving, joyful, patient, kind, good, faithful, gentle and self-controlled.[31] Read through the Old and New Testaments and you will see these seven attributes being displayed and talked about in relation to God. Read the Gospels and the life of Jesus and you will see the same displayed through Jesus. The very same things are planted in you by the Holy Spirit, and you begin to become the image of God again, as His redeemed child. Not God, but godly.

[31] Galatians 5:22-23.

Part Two

Deity

He is before all things, and in him
all things hold together.

Colossians 1:17

Chapter Seven

Tick, Tock!

Time. It is the most common commodity.

You have things that make you unique. Your family background dictates how you look. Everyone is born into different environments and various circumstances. You may have a highly paid job, or be currently unemployed. You may be married, single, widowed or divorced. Your language may be English or another, and of any one of hundreds of dialects and variations. You may be a child of God or not.

However, you have the same amount of time at your disposal as everyone else: 168 hours a week.

In the workplace your schedule can fill up rapidly. Even if you do not have a job where you need a diary, your day is still governed by how long a task may take, how long a journey may take, or how long a meeting may take. *Tick, tock! Tick, tock!*

My own life is full of appointments. My wife and I, as technology has moved on, now synchronise our diaries online. Our phones and tablets peep and chirp at us to get our attention when an appointment is added. Time is precious. There are regular scheduled activities in my diary, study time, team meetings, even prayer days! *Tick, tock! Tick, tock!* This generation has more labour-saving devices to free up more time than any previous generation. The hard work is now taken out of mundane tasks.

Soon after we purchased a house I ripped out the old kitchen and installed a new one. There was some degree of trepidation shown by my family as they had never seen me do any kind of DIY, but after a week there was the new kitchen, all gleaming and sparkling. I had left space for appliances including a dishwasher. Someone in the church actually gave us their old one, which was a great blessing, but next to all the newness in the kitchen this old, battered machine looked out of place. We did not mind; we had never had one before.

Shortly after the project was finished a visitor from church came to the door. Barbie was so excited. "Come and look at this!" she exclaimed and literally dragged them through the house towards the kitchen. I was expecting her to start praising my skills, the tiling, the floors, the new hob. "Look! I have a dishwasher!"

I was slightly deflated but then realised that having a young family with three sons, she hated the washing up. I guess no one loves it! She was happy because once a meal was over we could load the dishwasher and the home looked tidy again as it ran through its cycle. Ultimately she was excited about saving time.

You can save time, invest time, give time. You can never get back lost time. Despite all the things that you have to help, you may not seem to have enough time. You are networked, linked through social media, emails and cell phones, all of which take up time. Even as I write these words, having blocked out some diary time, I have had to put my cell phone on silent so I can check it later and avoid interruptions.

Why does God Take His Time?

Time is a matter of perspective. Time is viewed in the moment or retrospectively. Your life is a series of moments that become your history. You mark these in time.

Jesus is fully man and fully God. That means He is the only man in all of history who is not bound by time. Seated now with the Father,[32] He sees time from heaven's perspective. Like God, as part of the Trinity, He is transcendent – above all things. He is not bound to time, He is not bound by time, and He is not bound in time. He is timeless. Heaven marks time but lives outside of it. Perhaps this is why He is sometimes late according to your schedule! Yet Jesus

---

[32] Ephesians 1:20; Colossians 3:1.

chooses to live within your timeframe. He is not restricted by your time but lives therein. This is an exquisite paradox.

When Jesus was born He entered into Earth's timeframe, His humanity was subject to time. It was not the first occasion that the Godhead had entered chronological time. God walked with Adam in the cool of the evening in Genesis. Throughout the Old Testament there are epiphanies where God, and Jesus, existed in Earth's time whilst not being restricted by time.[33] Time is a creation of God, the Creator is never subject to the created. When Jesus came as a man He began to walk the earth in the same way Father did with Adam. Now that Jesus is seated at the right hand of God, it is the Holy Spirit who moves through the world, everywhere at once, in time and outside of time.

Yet answers to prayer still seem to come late.

Ever Present

Jesus promised the disciples that He would be with them, even until the end of the age.[34] The word 'age' is *aion* in the Greek text. It signifies a period of indefinite length or time in relation to what takes place in that period.[35] It is an all-encompassing phrase to describe the time in which the present earth resides, a time that will eventually end as God has planned. It is also a binding statement. Jesus is promising that although He is about to step outside of time, He is ever present within it. He is the only person to do this.

In Hollywood blockbusters God appears in all kinds of forms, stepping in and out of time, like a celestial Morgan Freeman. This is not true of the real God.

Passages in the Bible use anthropomorphisms, words giving Him human attributes, to describe Him. This is to help you understand His love and His character. Jesus says He is Spirit.[36] The Holy Spirit is exactly that too: Spirit. Jesus is the only one of the Godhead who

---

33 Psalm 139.

34 Matthew 28:20.

35 W.E. Vine, M.F. Unger, W. White; *Vine's Complete Expository Dictionary of Old and New Testament Words;* Thomas Nelson: London (1985).

36 John 4:24.

has human form, and will continue to have human form forever. He is the only member of the Trinity to have scars, from nails, a crown of thorns and a spear. When you reach heaven all your scars will be gone for Jesus is the only one who will carry marks of death that God has chosen never to erase.

As a man, Jesus intercedes for you. As a man, He sits at God's right hand. As a man, He remains in your time. As a man, the only man to do so, He also sees heaven's perspective. He is able to move between heaven and earth freely.

CHAPTER EIGHT

You're Too Late!

The anguish in their cries could be heard as Jesus walked towards the village.[37] The news had come forty-eight hours before that His friend was gravely ill. Hearing the news, Jesus stayed where He was for another two days.

The disciples had probably forgotten about the message concerning Jesus' friend in the busyness of the ministry they were engaged in. Two-day-old news is history. Living in the moment is more important for them. Suddenly, Jesus cuts short the teaching and says, "Let us go back to Judea. Lazarus is sleeping and needs waking up!"

Confused by this statement the disciples reply, "Sleep's good! Sick people need their rest; he'll be fine." It is only later they realise that Lazarus has actually died.

Jesus knew. The prayers had gone to the Father and the Father had now assigned Jesus to go.[38]

They walk for at least another two days to get to Bethany where the family stay.[39] The disciples are fearful of going; their last trip there did not go well and they are worried.[40] Thomas – who, you will recall, is labelled "doubting" as a nickname throughout Christian

---

37 Read John 11 for the account for the resurrection of Lazarus.

38 John 5:19.

39 We know this because the news came two days before and Martha tells Jesus he's been in the tomb two days.

40 John 8:59, 10:31, 11:8.

history – seems to be the only one with some faith to follow. He says, "Let's go, too, that we may die with Him!" True, intonation is not heard as you read the Scriptures, but surely if he were doubt-filled or fearful he would have said, "I'll wait here until you get back!" What he is expressing is that life is not worth living without Jesus. He would rather die with Him than live without Him.

If this is understood about Thomas perhaps he should not get such a hard time when, overwhelmed with grief, he struggles to accept what the others know to be true for they have all seen the resurrected Jesus. Think about that... Jesus says that those who believe and yet have not seen Him are the blessed ones. Whom is He talking about? Not the eleven disciples; they have all seen Jesus. He is talking about every believer who has believed in His name throughout the centuries who have not seen Him. He's talking about you.

There have been many miraculous sightings of Jesus through the millennia – those who have died and returned to tell us of heaven and who have had visions of Jesus. Sometimes these saints are portrayed as the ultimate in faith or superhero believers. Their stories encourage and add to the hope Christians profess. They are not the blessed ones though. That's you! To believe and not see is the essence of faith.[41]

As they approach, the wails of the mourners can be heard. When someone dies in a small place like Bethany, especially someone before their time, the whole village mourns. Bethany, being only two miles from Jerusalem, is close enough for many to come and mourn with Mary and Martha; the place is heaving with grief.

Jesus' heart begins to break. These are His friends. He feels their pain. Hearing that Jesus is on the way, Martha rushes out to see Him; Mary is too disconsolate to leave the house.

Anger! Rage! *It's your fault! You could have stopped this!* Denial and anger are companions in grief. Martha is not running to meet Jesus and celebrate His arrival. She is mad! *Why didn't you come when the message was sent? Do you think we would have bothered you if it wasn't serious?*

You're too late! Martha lets Jesus have it all, full blast, both barrels. Even in her despair she still manages to rally some faith in

---

41 Hebrews 11:1.

God: "But I know that even now God will give you whatever you ask."

How bad is your situation? Does it feel like God is running late? Has the moment passed when you felt you needed Jesus' intervention?

Martha has faith in the providence of God. One day Lazarus will rise again, in the resurrection to come.

In the midst of your griefs and woes there is always eternal hope. The story does not end with your chapter. You are part of a greater work, a bigger picture, in which the Father works out the mysteries of the universe with perfect timing and precision. There is always hope, even though it is the hope of the future. This was Martha's hope.

It's Not Over

Jesus says some of the most famous words of Scripture which, ironically, we read at funerals! "I am the resurrection and the life!" All future hope is found in the present Jesus. He is telling her, "I am! I am God. I'm not late."

When you think of the future answers to your prayers you need to look to the present Jesus. He is the resurrection and the life for what you are facing. He feels the pain that you feel. So why does He seem so remote at times? As I read and re-read the account in John 11, I was struck by the fact that Jesus did not go all the way to their house. He remained outside of the village. This is so counter-cultural and breaks with the norm; the mourners would have thought this was a sign of dispassionate detachment. Aloof and separated. Do you ever feel Jesus has not entered into your situation but stands outside of it?

I have come to realise that Jesus does not always accept the invitations that I send Him to join my pity parties. Sometimes He does. He intervenes, overwhelms me with peace, takes care of the crisis. Other times not. When He does not, it is not to cause pain or hardship. It is to increase the trust that I have in Him.

If Jesus had entered the village and gone to the house, what He needed to say to Martha may have been lost in the din of the grieving process. Sometimes it's hard to hear what Jesus is saying to you over the noise of those around you who seem to know better, who 'understand' how God works, and how we should respond. Their voices can be deafening. Good friends will walk with you through your griefs, not criticise your lack of faith or presume to speak for God.

I was once helped by a member of the church I was pastoring at that time, who gave me a prophetic word. In a picture, she had seen me standing in front of the church and everyone was talking, giving opinions, talking over me. I also had a telephone at each ear and various handwritten messages for me that were being left by people on the pulpit. What did this mean? It did not make too much sense at the time. I came to realise that sometimes we have to remove ourselves and seek out some solitude to hear from God, without the opinions of others. Once we have heard from Him, we can seek their opinions on what has been said; not before. I have been pastoring churches long enough now to realise that not everyone's opinion is based on the Bible. Some seek those who will merely support them.

Jesus does not always support our opinion or attitude. He does what the Father does. He takes us to a place of healing, by helping us confront the pain, with Him.

Left Alone in a Crowd

Where's Mary? She has stayed home. On their last meeting the roles of these two sisters seem to be reversed. Luke 10:38-42 describes how the two sisters opened their home to Jesus.

You will remember that Martha busily prepares a meal and criticises her sister's negligence of the duties at hand. How can Jesus allow Mary to sit and listen to His teaching? This is not the role of a woman in their culture. Jesus redresses the balance and assures Martha that not only is this alright, but that Mary has chosen something that will not be taken from her.

Do not cook Jesus meals that He did not ask for! Life is busy with ministry, work, church activities and the like. None of these things are bad; they need doing. (Someone was going to have to cook a meal for the guests at some point. Just not now.)

The friendship grows between Jesus and this family. When they are in crisis they call for His help. Mary, though, having listened to Jesus' teaching previously, when she hears He is near, stays at home. It may have been her grief that overwhelmed her but it should be remembered that faith is not faith unless it is tested. Without the crucible of difficulty, faith is merely wishful thinking.[42]

When faith is tested Martha shows the genuineness of hers; Mary shrinks back. All of us can be heroes of faith one moment and deniers of Jesus the next. None are immune. Jesus calls us all to a place outside of the moment. A place for Him to work in the heart.

To be fair to Mary, there may have been so much going on around her that she did not realise that Jesus was nearby. Maybe she had not noticed Martha slip away. In the midst of the corporate mourning it can be very difficult to take note of who is missing. When Martha comes and tells her that Jesus is there she gets up quickly and goes to Him. In the midst of your trial, get up quickly and go to Him! Don't delay. Figuring everything out on your own will only add to your anxiety. The answer does not lie within the trial but in the One who is above it.

Remember the professional mourners? They seem to have cornered Mary, surrounding her, reflecting and magnifying her tears. It may be her anguish was more public than her sister's. They do not seem to notice, or even care, that Martha has left. Seeing Mary's haste, they go after her, assuming that she is on the way to the tomb to mourn there.[43]

People around you will assume all kinds of things are going on when they are not. Again, their opinions can be misleading and their advice contrary to what Jesus needs of you.

They go with her to continue the grieving process at the tomb. It has been four days. Maybe Mary has done this every day. Her urgency compels them to follow.

When you're in the middle of a testing situation it is important not to forget the influence you have over others. I do not mean that you have to put on a brave face and be stoic for the sake of others. There have been too many in the Church who hide their true circumstances behind the Sunday morning smile. Some believe that showing any sign of a chink in our armour or stress would be interpreted as a sign of weakness. Church should be the one place

---

[42] 1 Peter 1:6-9.

[43] John 11:31.

where weaknesses and your reliance on God are acknowledged, where mutual encouragement and support is demonstrable.[44]

Remember His strength is made perfect in your weakness. It is in fragility that your reliance, and your acknowledgment of your need of Him, grows. When others see you respond to God's grace in this way they too will follow, breaking the pattern and mould of their own old, well-worn behavioural responses at the same time.

Tears of God

Arriving where Jesus is, Mary falls down and weeps. Her riposte is the same as Martha's. "If you'd been here he'd still be alive!" The anguish is there, the same pain, the same accusation. Jesus does not repeat the same conversation with her though. Perhaps this is because He already taught her that He is the resurrection and the life when she sat at His feet before. He tells us what we need when we need it. In this case He simply asks, "Where have you laid him?" and they tell Him.

The shortest verse and one of the most widely known phrases of the Bible is found right here. It encapsulates a moment in time, displaying for all to see that Jesus feels the pain of those around Him. More than this, it shows that Jesus *feels pain*. It is real for Him too.

Jesus wept.

Simple words on the page in your Bible. The gravitational pull of this nine-lettered phrase has been drawing people back to this passage of Scripture for nearly two thousand years. These words provide comfort for you as you realise that Jesus hurts too. He is not alien to your tears, your pain. He suffers as a human being, fully God, fully man. Exquisite, the most highly prized One, yet displaying human frailty. These words provide hope.

How many times have you read that Jesus was moved with compassion before a great miracle took place? Compassion is not just an isolated act of will but also an emotional response to a need. It becomes the imperative in the crisis. Many Christians will claim to have compassion but don't. They prefer a gospel where nothing ever goes wrong in life and, if it does, it has to be because of sin or a lack of faith in the part of another Christian. They will quote at you,

---

44 2 Corinthians 12:9; 1 Thessalonians 5:11.

"And we know that in all things God works for the good of those who love him, who have been called according to his purpose," without empathy.[45] Without tears. Without love. They may quote a truth of Scripture in a truth-denying way. Never forget, mourn with those who mourn.[46] There will come a time for the other promises of God to be declared. Jesus did not condemn their hurt. He hurts too. He does not condemn your hurt; He hurts with you.

Jesus wept. Not as a sign to others. He was experiencing His own grief. This is a paradox. He is the resurrection and the life. He is about to perform a miracle. Jesus lives in the moments with you.

Some understood this. "See how he loved him!"[47] Sadly, in secularised culture there are some who would try and use Bible verses like this out of context to prove that Jesus was homosexual in orientation to justify their own practices. They miss the point that Jesus is grieving by using *eisogesis* – placing one's own biases, presuppositions and agendas into the text.

Exegesis seeks to see what the text says, in the context of what is happening based on careful analysis of the culture and meaning to its original readers, and then seeks truths that span the millennia that will help you live right today.

Exegesis means to 'lead out of'. In context, Jesus is grieving. Period. I find it reassuring that when I cry, Jesus feels it. I find great comfort in knowing that Jesus, who flung stars into space and by whom all things are held together, weeps and mourns with me at my low times.

Too Cynical to Notice

There are always cynics too. There were those who sneered and said Jesus could heal the blind but not stop someone from dying. They mocked Him in His pain. There are always going to be these kinds of people in the world and in your life. Ignore them. Jesus did not give a counter argument. He didn't get distracted. He moved forward.

---

45 Romans 8:28.
46 Romans 12:15.
47 John 11:36.

Remember, though, that people are not disposable, no matter who they are. Jesus still died for them. He died for His friends and His enemies.

One of the things that has been popularised by social media, possibly as an unintentional side effect, is the growing circulation of pithy sayings dressed up as posters, displayed as truth and posted online. Some of these are posted by Christians as biblical truth. These mantras will say things like, "If your friend hasn't called you and been in touch, they are not your true friend." More subtly, "A true friend is always there for you when you're low." Or even, "If a relationship is one-sided, ditch it!" Is it just me or can you see the underlying selfishness in these statements? The idea is that you are the centre of the universe and people are there to serve you. If they don't, move on. It is true that some relationships are unhealthy and destructive. What kinds? Obviously where there is abuse.

People who believe these kind of statements are cynical. Jesus did not engage during His weeping with the cynics. But he still died for them. Aren't you eternally grateful that when you were cynical and contemptuous of Jesus, He still died for you?[48] Do not dispose of people quickly; they are not replaceable. Follow Jesus' example. Everyone will see the miracle; not everyone will understand it.

Arriving at the cave where they have laid Lazarus to rest, Jesus is deeply moved again. We can assume that He is still weeping.

Jesus is now outside the tomb. Often in your life Jesus will take you back to the place where you last faced a situation of difficulty. Life at times appears to be cyclical. You will have seen it in others; the woman who goes from relationship to relationship only to find that each new man is physically abusive; the man who constantly eats and overeats in stressful situations and battles with his weight. There will be cycles in your life too. It doesn't matter what they are.

People do not always learn from their mistakes. A mistake without learning the lesson soon becomes a pattern. In life there will be lessons that you have learnt at a school that God never enrolled you in. To help overcome this, Jesus will take you to a place to confront the grief.

---

[48] Romans 5:8.

In John 11:38-44 the account of Lazarus' resurrection is recorded. Within this you begin to see that there are things that He tells you to do and things He does that you cannot do for yourself.

Roll Away the Stone!

Let's uncover the real issue here. Let's go deeper. It's great to have a Saviour who understands our griefs; it's another to realise that He wants to uncover the secret things in our lives.

Martha questions Jesus' sanity! "Jesus, you're too late. *Tick, tock!* He will stink by now. Jesus, don't you know that the result of death is decay, and with decay comes a stench? Death has a smell and it's not one to savour. Jesus, it's enough that you have empathised with our grief. Coming and standing by the grave to show your respect is enough. It's made up for your poor timekeeping and even the delayed answer to our message to come. You're here now; that's enough."

Jesus lives in the moment with you to help you see the eternal picture. Your hope in Jesus must not just be that you will be taken up out of this world one day but that He changes the world in which you live.

Remember What He Said

"Did I not tell you that if you believed, you would see the glory of God?" Remembering what He said takes us to a place of trust. He has told Martha that Lazarus will rise again, but she has interpreted this through her 'one day' theology. He told the disciples that He was going to wake Lazarus up. Only later will they understand what He meant. Maybe the light is dawning on them now as they watch and see what is unfolding before them.

Jesus has told the disciples that Lazarus needs waking up! Remembering what Jesus has said means that you have something to pray! You can remind Him of His promises to you. This should not be some kind of blab-it-and-grab-it prayer. It should be a deep and earnest petitioning of Jesus: you promised X, my experience is Y, please honour your promise. He is faithful and true.[49]

---

[49] Psalm 33:4; Revelation 19:11.

So you have to roll away your stone. That takes courage. It takes courage to face the same thing again in your life where there has been past failure. It takes courage to remember what Jesus has said and believe Him against all the odds. The first things that have to be done to turn the difficulty in your life around sit within your power. *Roll away the stone.* Most people will not take these two steps of obedience because Martha is right: the air is now filled with the pungency of death's victory. Mixed with their grief and their faith is the overwhelming reminder of what has been lost.

How many things in your life have turned rotten before Jesus intervenes?

Rely on Jesus' Prayers

Jesus prays at this burial site. He breathes deeply and speaks loudly enough to be heard. When death is breathed in by the Life, death dies. He looks up and says, "Father, I thank you that you have heard me. I know that you always hear me, but I said this for the benefit of the people standing here, that they may believe that you sent me."[50]

Read those words again. Why did it take the death of a loved one for the two sisters to believe? Why does it take some major incident or crisis in life for people to turn to God? It's not always the case, true. Did God let Lazarus die? If He did it was only so He could be raised.

Jesus could have just commanded the corpse to live immediately. He didn't. He prays. He prays for the benefit of those who are listening. He prays that they will know that Father God has sent Him.

There is a powerful dynamic here. Do not pray as though summoning Jesus. The sisters did just this; they sent for Him. Jesus didn't respond to that. He responded when God sent Him.

Remember that whilst many were healed during Jesus' earthly ministry, people still died in Israel during the same period. Not everyone would call for Him. Some died and Jesus merely comments on it.[51] Bad stuff still happened when Jesus walked the earth. Calling

---

[50] John 11:41-42.
[51] Luke 13:3.

for Him is so important. Faith brings hope. Jesus, when receiving the summons, would have prayed about when to go, if at all.

The quality and depth of Jesus' prayer life outstrips that of yours or mine. There are instances when Jesus would take Himself to a place of solitude to pray and commune with Father.[52] These prayer times seem most important to Luke, out of all the Gospel writers, as he recounts more of them than the others. For Luke, this is an outstanding feature of Jesus' ministry. When Jesus was baptised, Luke explains that it was whilst Jesus was praying that the Spirit descended.[53] It is Luke who records that Jesus took Peter, James and John to pray on a nameless mountain that is now called Transfiguration. This gives an idea of what happens when Jesus prays: heaven opens!

Jesus is still praying for you; as a man, a human intercessor, right now, this moment, this second.[54]

The Bible describes Jesus as your mediator. This means a 'go-between' taken from the Greek word *mesites*, being a combination of two words meaning 'middle' and 'to go'. This description shows Jesus moving between two parties, God and humanity, to bring peace.[55]

This is played out in the account of the resurrection of Lazarus. The attributes of divinity are being displayed as well as Jesus' total reliance upon the Father for guidance.

"Father, I thank you that you have heard me. I know that you always hear me..." This is a statement of divinity. Obviously God hears every prayer that is prayed when it is prayed. There is a scene in the film 'Bruce Almighty' in which Jim Carrey's character, being given the ability to hear every prayer, resorts to sorting these on email and then simply answers yes to all. Everyone has a simplistic understanding that God hears prayers. Jesus is not just saying, "God, you hear." He is saying, "Because we are one, you hear every

---

52 Matthew 26:36; Mark 1:35, 14:32; Luke 3:21, 5:16, 6:12, 9:18, 9:28, 11:1.

53 Luke 3:21.

54 1 Timothy 2:5.

55 W.E. Vine, M.F. Unger, W. White; *Vine's Complete Expository Dictionary of Old and New Testament Words;* Thomas Nelson: London (1985); Mediator.

thought, every prayer and see every action." Remember, Jesus said He only does what He sees the Father doing.[56]

Jesus' prayer continues, "...but I said this for the benefit of the people standing here, that they may believe that you sent me." He is saying, "They need this! They need this miracle! Right now in the midst of their despair and anguish. They need the change to come now!" How did Jesus know this? Because He's the mediator, fully man, fully God. Only by possessing both deity and humanity could He comprehend the claims of the one and the needs of the other.[57] Jesus knows this because He is experiencing their despair and is able to petition the Father. To what end? To meet a need? No. To bring glory to the Father. When the Father is glorified, needs are met. When needs are met, the Father is glorified. The egocentric nature of society wants you to believe that it's all about you, what you deserve, your desires. It's not. It's about Him. When His name is glorified your needs will be met. Jesus stands uniquely placed to mediate and pray on your behalf. Remember He is praying for you!

Rejoice at His Command

The crescendo arrives: "LAZARUS, COME OUT!"

A palpable silence hangs in the air as Jesus' words echo in the cave, people craning and straining to gain a better view. Silence as Lazarus' decaying skin and tissue are recreated. Silence that is slowly interrupted as a shuffling sound can be heard as linen-clad feet make their way to the entrance of the cave.

In a matter-of-fact way John records what happens next: "The dead man came out."

Shock. Silence of a new kind envelopes the crowd as they stare in disbelief.

Sometimes the commands of the Lord seem delayed. It is not that the power of Jesus is insufficient. In the spiritual realm the change happens instantly. In the natural realm the change takes time to occur. In Lazarus' case it did not take long, but would have taken

---

[56] John 28:29, 10:34-38, 14:31.

[57] W.E. Vine, M.F. Unger, W. White; *Vine's Complete Expository Dictionary of Old and New Testament Words;* Thomas Nelson: London (1985); Mediator.

some time for tissues to regrow, even miraculously, and for him to make his inhibited way out of the cave. When you are desperate for an intervention from heaven even this delay can seem unbearable. Perseverance through the appearance of heavenly inactivity is vital. Do not give up.

When I became a Christian I heard a lot of testimonies about God waiting until one minute to midnight before He answered prayers. It's almost as though theological thought would allow God to take time but never be late. The resurrection of Lazarus shows that God has a different clock; it's sometimes five minutes *past* midnight, but Jesus is ever present. It's never too late. Rejoice when the command has left the lips of the Lord.

Reveal the Promise

Such is the dumbfounded nature of the crowd that Jesus has to tell them to do the obvious: untie him. There underneath the grave clothes was Lazarus with baby-like new skin!

One of the things that Jesus cannot do for you is to live in the promise He has given you. It's up to you to live in the new reality that He has given. A few moments before, the sisters were mourning the loss of their beloved brother. Now they are going home as a family again, all together, laughing, questioning, believing afresh in the wonders of their God.

For some they never reach this point in their faith. It's as though their Lazarus has been raised, but they have never taken off the grave clothes, and so they have a resurrected promise fettered by death-stained bindings in their lives, hobbling around trying to act normally, but still dressed for a funeral! Take off the grave clothes.

There are things that Jesus will want you to do in your desperate moments: rolling away your stone; believing in your Saviour; unwrapping your promise. There are things that He will do: interceding for you; commanding the dead thing to live; instructing you to take off the funeral clothes. He is always present. He lives in your time but with heaven's clock. He is wonderful. He is exquisite.

Chapter Nine

Jesus Changes Everything!

Jesus changes everything. You may think that everyone who encounters Jesus becomes an incredibly loyal follower. Sadly, this is not always the case. Jesus Himself likens the Kingdom to a farmer who scatters seeds; some fall on the path and are trampled and eaten by the birds; some fall on rocks and begin to grow but due to lack of deep roots they cannot get moisture; some fall on good soil and grow to yield a crop up to a hundred times that which is sown.[58] If you are reading this book you are definitely in the last group, for those who do not develop their spiritual lives will have no interest in personal growth and, therefore, will not read.

The aim of the farmer is to seed the good soil. The farmer is not aiming for the rock or the pathway when he scatters his seed, but it is inevitable that some will land there.

This was clearly illustrated for me at a Carol Service. The church had been encouraged over the previous twelve months to prayerfully consider whom they would bring to the Christmas services. We did this through a simple initiative called one-plus-one. The idea is not original to us but seemed to work well in our church culture. People prayed for their friends once a day, chatted to them once a week (at least), had a meal or coffee with them once a month, and invited them to church once a year. People in the church began to speak about their "plus ones". During the year we saw people come to faith

---

[58] Luke 8:5-6.

and visit the church. The crescendo of this was to be the Carol Service, for even in a Jesus-illiterate England there is still a willingness to go to a good Christmas service if invited. We planned it well. We made sure there was a good blend of the contemporary and the traditional. The lighting was just right and a living room was created on the stage, complete with a couch, fireplace, Christmas tree and toy cat! When the time came to deliver the message, I sat on the arm of the leather sofa, kept things succinct, but outlined the gospel. When it came to the appeal, we asked people to raise their hands and eleven people responded. To some this may not seem very many. To others you would long to see this happen in your church. Admittedly, we had become used to maybe five or six people publicly responding in a gospel meeting; for eleven to say they needed Jesus was double what we would have anticipated.

Three things struck me about this night. Firstly, although we worked really hard at making sure the service was good, it was not the lights, staging or singing alone that brought people to faith. Secondly, people will respond when they are challenged. The seed needs to be thrown. There were certainly more than eleven people who had not met with Jesus in the church building that evening. Thirdly, and this is the most important point, when I spoke with those who responded afterwards, all of them, every single last one, had been witnessed to and brought to the church that Christmas by a friend who had prayed for them once a day, spoken with them once a week, met with them once a month and had invited them to church. We had prepared the fallow ground as best we could. Although this was exciting, not all of them have come through into a living faith. This is perplexing.

Healed, not Changed[59]

Occasionally there would be a fracas as someone tried to take his spot. He was well known to the other regulars there. He'd been there for most of his life, ever since the accident. It had ruined him, meant he could not walk even a few feet, could have no hope of employment, and meant he had been abandoned to this place by his family. Occasionally people would be kind as they walked past,

[59] John 5:1-15.

throwing money or a scrap of food. Most were indifferent, ignoring the slowly decaying invalid as he lay with his lifelong possessions, such as they were, hoping for someone to help when the waters began to stir. Some said an angel came and moved the waters. Others claimed it was a god, the name of which he could never recall.[60] He wondered if it were a myth, if he had wasted his hope of health on the superstitions of others; after all, he could not remember anyone being healed there, just rumours.

There was a camaraderie here. There were many in the same situation. Some were like him, unable to walk. Others were blind. Some had seizures. They cared for each other through the years; grew to know each other. Suspicious of outsiders in their little community, unless they could help them with money, food or to get to the water before anyone else, they were a band of brothers.

This place was a place of healing, near the Sheep Gate of Jerusalem, called Bethesda.[61] He would often ponder that name: House of Mercy. Mercy seemed to be in pretty short supply from his perspective. The name conjured up all manner of lovely pictures, but actually, for him, this was a hot, smelly, unsanitary place. The waters were not particularly clean; people washed in them too.

Days rolled into nights and nights into days in this tiresome place. Leaving was not an option; he could not afford to miss when the waters gave up their healing powers. He had been there thirty-eight years. Most, if not all, of the old-timers had since died at the side of the pool. He could not work out if he were the longest serving member of this forgotten club, but he knew he was a veteran, a pillar in this community. Such status did not curry any favours when the waters moved. Bedlam would break out. Some would drag themselves towards the water's edge. Others had family or friends who would regularly visit and, if their visit coincided with the healing time, they would carry their loved ones into the pool in the hope that they would be restored. Pushed aside, trampled, forgotten, this band of brothers turned mercenary when there was even the slightest glimmer of this misery ending.

---

[60] See note (i) in 'Additional Notes' on page 240.

[61] See note (ii) in 'Additional Notes' on page 240.

A shadow interrupted his thoughts. A man had stopped and was looking at him. Expectantly, he stretched out his dirt-encrusted hand in hope of a few coins for food. The man stepped closer and sat beside him, looking around at the sight before them.

The silence grew until this visitor asked, "Do you want to get well?"

Who is this stranger? Perhaps he is here to help. Maybe the prayers I have prayed have been heard. Of course I want to be healed!

Years of loneliness are formed into one sentence: "I have no one to help me when the waters are stirred; I am pushed aside." In that sentence is the answer, "Yes, I want to be healed." There is also hope that this new face is here to carry him into the waters, to push others out of the way.

He did not quite hear what the stranger said next. He heard the words but they were forgotten in the moment as power jolted through his crumbled frame and feeling returned to his legs. Sensations washed over him as nerve endings fired to life, limbs straightened and he could feel his feet for the first time in nearly four decades; the coarse texture of the blanket underneath him, muscles twitching and strengthening, toes flexing and moving. What had he said? "Get Up! Pick up your mat and walk!"

He was standing and hadn't even realised it. His view had changed; he had never seen the baths from this perspective, standing as an adult. Others were looking at him! How could this be? Were their eyes playing tricks upon them? Was this really their friend?

He looked around, but the stranger had melted away. Rolling up his mat, his home of years, he walked out of his nightmare. Finding his bearings – things had not changed that much but he was still disorientated – he walked forward wondering what life would hold.

Life was full of hope. Until he met the religious. It was the Sabbath and he was breaking the law, carrying his bed. A life filled with hopelessness is used to critical words; it is a default setting. His only defence was that the man who had healed him had told him to do it.

The Jews demand to know who would even suggest breaking the law on the Sabbath; telling someone to carry their mat, effectively to work on the Sabbath, is bad enough, but to actually carry out medical treatment on the Sabbath is even worse.

He thinks for a moment. It is only then he realises he has no idea who this enigmatic visitor was. He did not recognise him. He was not a relative of one of the regulars at the pool side.

They let him go; his own transgression forgotten. It seemed that they were interested in the healer more than the healed one. He walked up the steps, each one taken with a joy that no one else could understand, for most would take the action of taking one step after another for granted. He could not remember the last time he had been here. He was sure it was with his father, long since deceased. It was the Sabbath and it just seemed the right thing to do, to go to the Temple. He was not sure if it was God who had healed him. No one seemed to know. He had been banned from this place due to his disability and was going to at least see it again, perhaps offer a prayer of thanks to God, but certainly show himself to the High Priest so that he could be declared fit to worship and work. Tomorrow he would have to begin looking for a job. His previous source of income was no longer open to him.

He sensed Him at his shoulder before he saw Him. It was the stranger. People seemed to know Him. They were watching Him, listening to them.

"You're healed. You're well!" His smile was broad, His eyes sparkling. Lowering his tones just enough so that others could not hear, his magnetic eyes fixed on him: "Now, stop sinning; worse could happen if you don't!"

Worse! What could be worse than the years spent in the House of Mercy? He enjoyed his healing, but not the conviction of his own sin in the presence of the Holy One. He knew who this was. This was Jesus! He'd heard of Him. He went immediately to tell the Jewish leaders. Maybe there would be some reward for the information. He had heard they were building a case against Jesus; it was all he had heard about in the Temple courts. A new teacher, a dangerous man; *stay away from Him.* Walking on his newly healed legs he began a journey away from Christ.

Why Him?

When Jesus entered Bethesda He could have talked with anyone, healed anyone. Philip, Andrew, Peter, and probably Nathanael, were all from Bethesda and all would have known the locals. Maybe one of these disciples pointed the man out to Jesus because John's retelling highlights that He learnt of the man's condition. It is clear that Jesus sought the man out. Firstly, he went to him at the pool.[62] He then found him in the Temple. Jesus was always seeking the lost. He still is.

The Absurd Question

On the face of it, Jesus asks the obvious question: "Do you want to get well?" Why does He even ask? The man has been there thirty-eight years. That's a long time to wait. The waters would have been regularly stirred, especially as they were most likely caused by an intermittent spring.[63] Simple multiplication would mean that if these waters bubbled once a week then our protagonist would have had just under two thousand opportunities to be healed. No one would help him though. Why not sit nearer the edge of the pool so he could just roll in? Perhaps in the early days he had, although by his own testimony it seems he had never made it into the water.

Jesus understands the soul better than anyone. He knows that beyond the physical condition of this man is a sickness of the heart, a weakness of the inner man that he has become subjected to over time. Jesus also knows that it is possible to become institutionalised by your circumstances. If all he has known is that which is around him, perhaps he does not want to actually be well, for leaving everything that is familiar will take more faith than being healed. This does not mean that every person who has a long term illness does not want healing; but sometimes people become so adept at living with a condition and adapting their lives to it that it can be impossible to think of life without it.

You will have met those who are ill who actually become experts in their illness, sometimes knowing more than their own doctor on the subject. I am a diabetic and so have what some have called an invisible disease. I know my symptoms well and also have read a lot about it, talked with other diabetics about their experience, and have even been asked to talk with those newly diagnosed with the disease.

---

62 John 5:6.
63 J. Michaels, John Ramsey, NIBC, Paternoster Press: Carlisle (1995); 88.

I know what it is like to manage an illness and, at times, to allow an illness to manage you. Do I want to healed? Yes. As I write, I am not.

This was not the only time Jesus asked this question.[64] He may ask you the absurd or obvious too. You may ponder why He would do such a thing. It is not to irritate you, to condemn you, nor to frustrate you. He wants you to understand your motives in asking. Saying, "Yes, I want be healed," will have implications for you. It will mean having to make choices. Choices about how you live life from here on in. Choices about whether to return to work; for some leaving the welfare system they have depended upon for so long can seem impossible.[65]

I know that from personal experience. My mother, who was a single parent for many of my teen years, did not work after 1979. This meant that we struggled and lived on State benefits. For the most part I was grateful for this help. There were times when this was embarrassing though. She would apply for grants for clothing and get referred to a local charity for help. This meant going and selecting an outfit to wear that, in my mind, consisted of a dead man's clothes. Living on State welfare in this way can be demoralising. In this mix of all this was a definite apathy in the family. My mother was the daughter of a Romany Gypsy, Linda, and a car mechanic, Eddie. This mix of cultures had some implications for my mother, an only child, one of which was an inherent ability to talk her way out of most things and a dislike for work.

As I grew up I found myself with a constant battle of wanting to work but not being always able to beat the sense that the State should look after me. I was inherently lazy. This came to a head in the early years of my marriage. We had a son and I had been made redundant. Living in South Africa at the time, where there was no State help for me, this became a great internal struggle. As one month rolled into

---

64 Matthew 20:29-34; Mark 10:51; Luke 18:41.

65 One of the greatest blessings about being living in the UK is the developed welfare system and benefits that those in need can receive. This is our country's great strength, that the poor are helped. It is also a great weakness. Some, a minority, abuse this system and become professional benefit claimants. Sometimes, through no fault of their own, people can become trapped in this system and find it hard to break out. After a period of time it becomes easier to remain on State benefits.

another and another, my wife took a second job. This was not my finest hour. At one men's group at church someone commented that I must be the laziest guy in the room to allow this to happen. That hurt, because whilst I was not working, I was trying. At the next month's meeting I took my rejection letters with me and had them pray I would find a job. My wife's family were critical too. After a year I had some counsel and some prayer ministry about this issue and broke off ties with the Romany heritage.[66] I felt God say I would never be unemployed again. Three days later I had a job.

This change was put to the test when we returned to the UK three years later. My mother met us at the airport. Reaching over the barrier I thought she wanted to hug me, but she handed me an envelope. I was a bit shocked so asked what it was. It turned out it was benefit claim forms she had pre-completed; they just needed my signature. As you read this, you are probably shocked but it was her way of showing love.

I explained what God had done in my life and that I was going to look for work the next morning. Barbie and I went to town the next day and I did apply for several jobs. After a few weeks I received a job offer from the first employer I had applied to, with more money than advertised and a company car. God had changed things for me. Instead of joy and excitement when I told my mother, she looked confused and perplexed. She could not understand why I would turn down so much money from the State, to which I was entitled, and go to work for only a little more.

To this day, apart from my time as a student, God has blessed me with paid work. I am now accused of being driven, although I do not view myself in that way. Certainly I am not the man that my wife married. I do remember that feeling of being institutionalised and conditioned to believe that this was the way things were and nothing was ever going to change that. On that level I can empathise with the man in the Gospel and the reason for Jesus' question. If you are healed a new way of living has to be found.

---

66 We were blessed to have a dear saint called Phyllis Greenslade in the same church as us. She was an octogenarian who would use public libraries to research every aspect of a person's spiritual heritage. The ministry she carried out was well thought through, prayerful and powerful. My wife and I owe this promoted sister a debt of gratitude.

There is something else in the question too; Jesus often connected healing with the forgiveness of sins. It is not that physical healing shows the forgiveness of sins, but rather that Jesus, when ministering to people, never did a half job.[67] His love is complete.

Just One Touch from the King…

…changes everything.[68] So the song goes.

As a Pentecostal pastor I believe in the miraculous touch of Jesus. I have seen Him work wonders, and sometimes the changes that come are instantaneous. I have also come to realise that change comes to those who accept Jesus and to those who are touched by Him but choose not to follow Him. What seems amazing to people of the Christian faith is that not everyone is going to praise Jesus for their healing. The point is that many are seeking their healing, not their Saviour. Healing is their goal, not to know the Healer.

Jesus is gracious; He heals those who love Him and those who don't. The healing of this man was to point him to Jesus. Although he walked away, this did not then negate the physical healing he had received. Jesus left him physically healed. He does not withhold compassion just because someone is going to throw it back at Him. Jesus is more secure about this than His Church. There were others who walked away from Jesus because the cost was too high or the teaching too hard.[69] He seems to be the least seeker-sensitive Saviour at times! This is because Jesus is seeking disciples, not followers, while often churches are seeking followers, not disciples.

One touch from the King will often make a follower, even for a short season. One touch from the King makes a disciple when that person touched wants to give the rest of their life to Him in devoted adoration. Those who have heard the gospel message or been healed may not come through to discipleship. Rocky ground is rocky ground. Discipleship is always a choice, whether you enter the Kingdom through a miraculous experience or through a process that

---

67 Matthew 9:1-8.

68 A resounding song by Godfrey Birtell that can be viewed at: www.godfreyb.com/chords_and_lyrics.html.

69 Matthew 19:16-30; John 6:60-70.

is intellectually rigorous. There are no robots in the Church. The love of God is still unconditional.

Trampled by the Religious

In the parable of the sower, Jesus says that some seeds are lost through being trampled underfoot and eaten by the birds.[70] The way this tends to happen is that you meet someone straight after your miracle and they criticise you.

The Jews challenge the man for carrying his mat on the Sabbath. It will always be a question of law, tradition or what is simply acceptable for those who have not met with Jesus. The man does not admit his guilt. He passes the buck and blames Jesus. This might be some of what was in the heart of this newly healed man – not accepting responsibility for his own choices.

On a mission I was involved in in London, news came back to the team that a Muslim man had been healed in Trafalgar Square after prayer. We were excited to hear what was going to be said next; surely he had given his life to Jesus? Nope! He went on His way, healed. One day he will stand before God and, unless he has accepted Jesus, will have to give an account as to what he did with the healing God gave him. Shirking your responsibility here on Earth is one thing; you will not be able to do it for all eternity.

Jesus Keeps Seeking

John's retelling of the events does not end with healing; Jesus seeks the man out at the Temple. Because Jesus links healing with salvation. Because He does not do half a job. Because He loves this man so much He gives him another opportunity to repent.

> *Later Jesus found him at the Temple and said to him, "See, you are well again. Stop sinning or something worse may happen to you."* [71]

It is not that the man's predicament has been due to some sin. That was a popular belief at the time. In some circles of the Church it still is. Jesus made it clear that not all sin leads to an illness or

---

70 Matthew 13:4.
71 John 5:14.

physical impediment.[72] It is true that *some* sins can lead to physical symptoms. Paul tells the Corinthian church that sin surrounding the Lord's supper had led to sickness, even death.[73] Not all sicknesses show a sin root though.

It is equally true that a lack of faith does not lead to a lack of healing. Some would say that because Jesus said, "Your faith has made you well,"[74] that healing is linked to faith. You will have seen some pray for people and accuse them of having a lack of faith and that is why they are not healed. I find this abhorrent. It seems a great way to condemn those who already feel condemned. Faith is important but I think it is the continued faith in Jesus that is the real active ingredient here. Blaming people for a lack of faith in Jesus cannot explain why people of no faith are healed, why this man did not lose his healing when he rejected Jesus.

Jesus is ultimately rejected by this man. Instead of changing his ways he seeks out the Jews and tells them it was Jesus who healed him. No gratitude. No rejoicing. No thank you. No changed attitude. No fruit. Just healed.

The Bible tells us that Jesus spoke to him "later".[75] It is not clear if the man has gone straight to the Temple or has gone out and committed some long-awaited mischief; after all, he could not commit too many sins lying on a mat for thirty-eight years. Perhaps Jesus warned him because He could see there was no change in the man's heart, even though he could walk now.

Take comfort in the 'laters' of Jesus if you are praying for a loved one who seems to have met with Him and still no change has happened. Whilst there is an urgency to bring people to Jesus, for life is fragile and finite, Jesus will always seek them out later. He does not let go or give up.

John leaves the retelling hanging in the air; did worse happen to him? At that point is seems that he has made a decision not to follow Jesus. These things are in Father God's hands. He sees the heart. Trust that He will do the right thing.

---

72 John 9:1-12.

73 1 Corinthians 11:29-30.

74 Luke 17:19.

75 John 5:14.

PART THREE

Jesus' Sinlessness

For God was pleased to have all his fullness dwell in him, and through him to reconcile to himself all things, whether things on earth or things in heaven, by making peace through his blood, shed on the cross.

Colossians 1:19-20

Chapter Ten

He Stands When You Can't

'Everyone' Means You Too

Jesus is in the business of repairing the broken, defending the defenceless and bringing Creation back into right order. There is such richness in Colossians 1:20. "All things" speaks of the breadth of Creation. It simply tells us that *everything* will experience peace. We know Creation is groaning, waiting for that time when the peace of God rules again, fully, completely.[76]

"All things" also includes you: your situation, your life, your family, work, leisure, money and purpose. It may be that at times there is turmoil in life. It is frustrating to hear Christians condemning each other that there must be some sin in their life if there is trouble around them. Obviously if someone decides to walk a path in life or make decisions that are dishonouring to God, they cannot expect God's blessing and favour, although for a time all may seem well. Equally, it is unfair to say that those who are suffering have sinned in some way. Jesus said there would be trouble of all kinds in this world, but to take heart; He has overcome the world.[77] He reconciles you to God through forgiveness. To be forgiven is a marvellous thing! Forgiveness is brilliant! It is great to receive it and liberating. To be forgiven is to understand guilt. You may not feel guilty but that does not change the fact of guilt.

---

[76] Romans 8:22.
[77] John 16:33.

Confessions of an Offender

I was agitated and needed to get moving. The family were running late, including an additional teenager who was staying with us. They just seemed to have a plan of action to make me late for an important evening. Eventually I had them in the car, seatbelts on, and off we went, engine revs peaking and gears crashing in my medium-sized people carrier. Not designed for speed by the manufacturer, nor comfort either, the car resisted every attempt to make it go a little faster. I was late, a man of God on a mission, and was determined to get to our function on time.

I think he saw me coming. If not, he could certainly hear me. In an instant the policeman stepped out from behind a building, radar gun in hand, grimace on his face. *Brake!*

Too late. Ignominiously I was directed off the road to a car park where the questioning began.

Out of the car.

No, I have not been drinking.

Yes, I do know the speed limit.

Occupation: church minister.

Why in such a rush? We're going to an awards ceremony organised by the churches of the town to thank our refuse collectors and street cleaners for their work.

Smile, Keith, it might work.

"Sir, I have reason to believe that you are not telling me the truth and have been drinking. I am therefore going to administer a breathalyser test to confirm my suspicions that you are driving under the influence of alcohol."

Sniggers from the car. Children in the backseat are often amused at the embarrassment of adults. Raucous laughter from the front passenger seat where my wife could contain herself no longer at my embarrassment.

Eyebrows raised, a distinct lack of amusement from the police officer as he had me blow a steady and continuous breath into the machine.

All clear!

So you really are a pastor on your way to give prizes to public service employees?

Yes!

Relief. Vindication!

He understood my plight, could clearly see what I was having to contend with in the car, and a glimmer of sympathy crossed his otherwise expressionless face. "Well, you can be on your way as soon as I have written the ticket for speeding; you were four miles an hour over the limit!"

Four miles an hour! The public embarrassment of being breathalysed at the side of a busy road for four miles an hour! The entertainment value for the family for such a trifling bending of the traffic laws! Surely he could see my plight?

Whether I liked it or not, I was guilty. An offender. A law breaker. Poorer financially for the experience and the lesson learnt. I didn't feel guilty. How could I be? – I was on God's business! It did not seem fair.

Whether or not you feel guilty, if you have broken the law, you are. The law is black and white whilst, given the choice, a world of grey seems more palatable when you're accused of wrongdoing. It seems amazing that in those times of being found out, hundreds of reasons why it is not fair will come to mind. Guilt is not about perspective, how you feel, but about justice, what is right.

The policeman was right. I was guilty. I was speeding. I was embarrassed. I was caught. Nothing for it but to take the punishment. Protesting my innocence when I knew I was not would have only added to the punishment and having already set my family a bad example, I tried to take it gracefully. Unless a higher authority than the law came along, I was going to have to pay the fine.

Sure, I could have appealed to the courts, but I knew I was in the wrong.

Just Another Day[78]

She couldn't remember which day it was. Clients had come and gone, day had become night, night had become day. She was tired. Tired of life, tired of *her* life. It was a dangerous business to be in. Some men were kind, gentle even. Many were rough. There was no way out. He seemed nice enough; a new client, a bit bashful.

---

78 John 8:1-11.

Just as they were beginning, the door flew open and several men barged their way in, manhandling her out of the room. For a moment she was in shock as adrenaline rushed through her veins. Who were they? As they trailed her into the early morning light she knew: religious police! Pharisees and teachers of the law looking on, approvingly. Struggling against their grip, she saw her most recent and probably final customer melt away behind them.

Resistance would be futile as they began to frogmarch her towards the Temple for the trial. It would not take long. She began to wonder what paradise would be like. No, for her there would no heaven. No hope. At least this life would soon end. Her struggles would be over. Maybe Yahweh would be gracious.

Her hair fell over her swollen eyes as tears she could no longer hold back rolled down her artificially crimson cheeks. Standing before them, held in place by strong arms, she could hear the trial begin.

What would she say in her defence? Why hadn't they gone after one of the other girls? Why her? There were others far worse out there. She wondered about her new client. Was he bait? Why hadn't they arrested him?

In theory this scene could have been replayed many times a week, but in truth, she couldn't remember the last time this had happened. For her profession things were much safer under the Romans, although they were clients too, but only they had the right over who lived and died in Judea.[79] It was confusing too, as some of her accusers were people she recognised professionally.

Another Accuser?

Hush falls over the crowd as the nominated spokesman begins to list the charges.

Wait – he is not speaking to her. She shifts her gaze; whom are they talking to? Teacher? A new rabbi? Someone they know? Through matted hair and tears she sees Him, casual in his manner, unruffled, serene.

He seemed warm. Maybe it was the early morning sun or the fact that He was not looking at her accusers but at her. Men had been

---

[79] John 18:31-32.

looking at her for a very long time. She knew every look a man had. Lustful, condemning, hungry, even embarrassed. This was different. It was something she had never seen. It was compassion.

As she looked at him she was captivated by his eyes; the look of peace and grace overwhelmed her. Feeling a new confidence, she tried to focus on what they were saying: "...woman was caught in the act of adultery. In the law Moses commanded us to stone such women. Now what do you say?"

Even she knew the answer to this! Her mind flitted momentarily back to the client who had skulked away. He should be here too. They should both stand accused, both be judged, both be killed.[80]

Silence – as the words hung in the air.

Realisation began to dawn. This was not about her, although her fate seemed sealed; it was about this new rabbi. They were testing Him! It was a clever test too.

If He defends her then the Pharisees can claim He is a false messiah who does not follow the law. The whole incident could be a planned response to Jesus accusing them of not keeping the law.[81] They will now be able to show that Jesus too is a lawbreaker. Conversely, if Jesus agrees with them and condemns her to death they can report Him to the Roman authorities as a traitor to Rome who has taken Roman powers, setting Himself up against the empire; a capital crime punishable by crucifixion.[82]

She was the bait. She shifted her attention back to the nomadic preacher. She had heard of Him; this must be Jesus. There was no way out for Him either. If He answered wrongly then they could discredit Him as a false messiah.

He was ignoring them. Stooped on the ground, writing in the dusty floor, He was taking His time. She strained to see what he was writing.

Angered, the Pharisees harangued Him, repeating over and over the same question. He stood, turned and looked at them. Silence fell as they waited for His answer.

---

80 Leviticus 20:10.

81 John 7:19.

82 Check out the useful website agapebiblestudy.com for more on this insight.

"Let any one of you who is without sin be the first to throw a stone at her."

The Writing's on the... Floor

She heard Jesus' words and wondered what they meant. She braced herself for the first blow. She knew the Pharisees believed that they kept the law so intently that they were without sin.[83] They were always looking down on her.

Jesus had returned to His writing. She figured this would anger them. No one was allowed to write on the Sabbath unless it was not permanent.[84] The wind would blow away His writing; even in this Jesus was keeping the law.

She could feel the anger of the crowd begin to dissipate – firstly the older ones, then the middle-aged and finally the younger men. The young are often the last to recognise their shortcomings for their idealism has yet to be tested by life's experiences.

Silence.

The last few minutes had been filled with anger and hatred, not towards her, but towards Jesus. Perhaps her life had never actually been in danger although for her the experience was traumatic. They could not have killed her unless the Romans sanctioned it, to whom her crimes would have seemed petty. If they had entrapped Jesus she would have been forgotten and they would have had Him tried under Roman law.

She noticed Jesus looking again at her. Compassion came with words this time: "Woman, where are they? Has no one condemned you?"

"No one, sir," she said. She knew *He* could though! There was something hanging in the air, something in the answer He had given

---

83 Philippians 3:5-6 – Saul, later Paul, exemplifies this self-righteousness.

84 John 9:13-16 suggests that this day is the Jewish Sabbath. Writing was forbidden on the Sabbath unless the writing did not leave a lasting mark [Mishnah Shabbat 12:5]. Writing with fruit juice or in sand or dirt was permitted. We do not know if He was writing Scripture verses or the sins of the accusers but whatever He wrote His actions show that He did keep the law perfectly. Not only was the writing not permanent but the record of what He wrote was also not permanent.
Source: www.agapebiblestudy.com.

to the Pharisees. There was only one who could condemn her – the one without sin! The light dawned; this Jesus was sinless. He had the power to appeal, not to religious courts or Roman judiciary, but to His sinless self. He could condemn her!

His words washed over her as she felt the forgiveness she had craved for so long. "Then neither do I condemn you," Jesus declared. "Go now and leave your life of sin."

Her heart leapt. She had been forgiven! The sin had been acknowledged. He had told her to change, to leave the life of sin.

Jesus will never *ignore* sin. It is never condoned. He always *forgives* sin. He has not come to condemn the world but to save the world.[85]

She went home and cleaned house. She was now a follower of Jesus. Everything she was or would ever be were His.

Jesus Stands for You When You're Floored

Extraordinary in John's account is that the woman does not plead her innocence nor deny her guilt. When fully exposed to the crowd as to who she was, there was no denial, no plea for clemency, just the resignation of shame.

At times you cannot stand for yourself. People often protest to me, as a pastor, that God would not send them to hell for their behaviour. The truth is He does not send anyone to hell. The gospel is not that you are gay, or an adulterer, or a fraudster, a blasphemer or anything else and will thus be punished for that. The gospel is this: you were born into a fallen world and because all of humanity is separated from God due to the sin of the first Adam, all are destined for hell, but God has made a way back to Himself through Jesus Christ. All are born with an hereditary spiritual condition that means separation from God. It may not seem fair because you cannot do anything about it. God has intervened though. Something equally unfair is the death of the Innocent One for you.[86]

I have three sons. They are all exceptional young men and I love them dearly. I might know you and, if not, one day I might meet you; maybe we will never meet. Whether you are my friend, an

---

85 John 3:17.
86 John 3:16-18.

acquaintance, a stranger, I could never imagine sending any one of my three sons to die in your place. As much as I might like you, I do not have the capacity to love you more than I love my boys. Father God has done the impossible to bring you back to Him; He sent Jesus when you did not even know Him.[87]

Jesus stands for you when you cannot do so for yourself. He brings a reconciliation between you and God, restoring what is broken. He stands between you and those who would accuse you when you have no defence, no way out, no option but to accept the stoning that is coming your way. This is when the Lamb roars. You are His! You may have wronged people in the past, or even now. Do what is necessary to make it right. Apologise. Write the email or make the phone call to say sorry. You may have been wronged by others; forgive as Jesus has forgiven you.[88]

What is He Writing in Your Life?

Scholars have debated for centuries what Jesus could have written in the dust. Some have said the sins of those accusing the woman. Others, Scriptures that would nullify their accusations. Still others have postulated that he wrote something to the woman. One Christian comedian has said it was probably the names of their mistresses! What is known is that Jesus wrote, and that it was Jesus' spoken words, not his writing, that undid the crowd.

So why even mention that Jesus wrote in the dust? Is it just to show He was literate? Was He playing for time to come up with a strategy? Or was He illustrating something for her? Jesus regularly used visual illustrations in His parables, His storytelling. He told people to look at the fields, familiar roads, or caricatured the well-known religious leaders of the day.[89] Whatever He wrote, it had enough of an impact for her to stay after everyone left and for this incident to be in the Bible.

I like the idea of this silent communication, this personal assurance to the woman. We know that God writes too. He has

---

87 Romans 5:8.

88 Matthew 6:14-15.

89 John 4:35; Luke 10:30ff, 16:19ff.

something special written on His hands: your name![90] In heaven Jesus is not the only one who will bear marks. He will be the only one with *scars* on His hands, His feet, His side, his brow from the cruel crown of thorns. Father is marked too; He has written your name in His hands.

God writes. So Jesus wrote. I wonder – and I have no biblical basis to say this, so forgive my romanticism here – I wonder if He wrote her name? The name that would be in dust on earth but on the palm of God. Temporary on earth, permanent in heaven.

What is Jesus writing in your life? He is writing, in the broadest sense, the wider story of your life. That goes without saying. In the storm, in the moment when you cannot stand any longer and the stoning is imminent, what's He writing? He writes what you need to know.

Why Are You Not Zapped from Above?

There are those who receive their forgiveness with open arms and celebrations. They may have been forgiven a lot of things and so their joy is a hallmark of their salvation.[91] There are some who struggle to accept their forgiveness too. They struggle with the idea that Jesus has forgiven them. I am not talking here about those who cheapen the grace of Jesus by habitually, and knowingly, sinning. Such people use their liberty as an excuse for sin and have misunderstood the grace they have.[92] Jesus does forgive, but repentance is the key that unlocks this treasure from His heart.

I have lost track of the number of times people have sat with me and have said words similar to these: "If you only knew what I was really like, what I've really done, whom I've really hurt, you would understand that Jesus could not possibly forgive me!"

I normally answer this in two ways. Firstly, don't flatter yourself. You might think you are that bad; Paul claimed that prize long before you or I, and Jesus forgave Him.[93] Secondly, do you truly believe that the blood of Jesus has the same power today as it has always had?

---

90 Isaiah 49:16.
91 Luke 7:47.
92 Galatians 5:13.
93 1 Timothy 1:15.

For if you are that unique, that special, that talented to commit a sin that God has not thought of, then Jesus cannot actually be the Saviour of the whole world. There would be something lacking in His sacrifice and Father God's ability to transform a sinner's life. There isn't; you're in!

When I look over this incident in John's Gospel I find something that, at first, might be puzzling. Jesus seems to imply that the reason he does not condemn her is that no one else has.

> *Jesus straightened up and asked her, "Woman, where are they? Has no one condemned you?" "No one, sir," she said. "Then neither do I condemn you."*[94]

At first glance you could think that this means that Jesus is the last in the line on this journey to forgiveness. He isn't. He is making a point that she is already forgiven, therefore the accusers have no case against her!

When did this happen? When Jesus said, "If any one of you is without sin, let him be the first to throw a stone at her."[95]

He effectively said, "We all know only God can forgive this woman, so if you want to put yourself in His place go ahead, but as you are not God, and have sinned, jog on!"

Jesus' ability to give you access to the Father's love and forgiveness is not found in the quality or depravity of your sin. It is found in Jesus' perfection, His sinlessness, His divinity, His compassion and His sacrifice.

When He tells her that He does not condemn her either, there is more than just a relieved woman; there is a saved soul.

Why aren't you zapped from above for the sins you have committed or are currently committing? Because you live in the time of His grace. Jesus will always show us grace which, by its very nature, is not deserved. If you choose to refuse it, that's your choice. Encountering Jesus at the depth of sin and hopelessness brings life though. You are not punished now because Yahweh is not like the mythical god Zeus, portrayed as a white-bearded, lightning-bolt-

---

94 John 8:10-11a.
95 John 8:7.

throwing despot. Yahweh is gracious, forgiving, loving, patient and slow to anger.[96] Jesus is the same.

[96] Exodus 34:6.

PART FOUR

Jesus' Humanity

...and through him to reconcile to himself all things, whether things on earth or things in heaven, by making peace through his blood, shed on the cross.

Colossians 1:20

Jesus went out as usual to the Mount of Olives, and his disciples followed him. On reaching the place, he said to them, "Pray that you will not fall into temptation." He withdrew about a stone's throw beyond them, knelt down and prayed, "Father, if you are willing, take this cup from me; yet not my will, but yours be done." An angel from heaven appeared to him and strengthened him. And being in anguish, he prayed more earnestly, and his sweat was like drops of blood falling to the ground. When he rose from prayer and went back to the disciples, he found them asleep, exhausted from sorrow. "Why are you sleeping?" he asked them. "Get up and pray so that you will not fall into temptation."

Luke 22:39-46

CHAPTER ELEVEN

Virgin Birth

Larry King, the famed CNN talk show host, was once asked whom he would like to interview if he could choose from anyone from all of history. He answered, "Jesus Christ." When questioned regarding what he would ask, King replied, "I would like to ask Him if He was indeed virgin-born. The answer to that question would define history for me."[97]

For King, an avowed atheist, this question is the most important.

Science Speaks

In the 1950s the Lancet, the British Medical Journal, published a series of findings from research that sought to answer the question of whether parthenogenetic reproduction – that is, conception without sexual intercourse – was possible in humans. After experiments involving women who claimed no man had been involved in the conception of their offspring, the Balfour-Lynn study declared they had indeed discovered a genuine virgin birth. A later study questioned their findings, stating the methodology was questionable, therefore a virgin birth could not be concluded[98] and the study is inconclusive.

---

97 Ravi Zacharias, *Jesus Among Other Gods,* (W Publishing Group, Nashville, 2000), p31.

98 Eric R. Pianka; *Virgin Birth in Human Females?* http://www.zo.utexas.edu/courses/THOC/VirginBirth.html, accessed 28/04/15.

Science is silent on the possibility of a virgin birth for it has no evidence to support the possibility. To deride people of faith becomes easier for some.

It is *theoretically* possible for a woman to spontaneously conceive. Certain rare conditions would have to be in place to make this possible and the chances of these occurring outside of a modern laboratory are zero. For a woman to get pregnant without a male sexual partner or medical intervention, one of her eggs would have to produce, on its own, the biochemical changes indicative of fertilisation and then divide abnormally to compensate for the lack of sperm DNA. That's the simple part! In fact, these do happen; these two events occur in the eggs or egg precursor cells of one out of every few thousand women.

That in itself does not lead to offspring. The egg would need to be tricked into thinking a male sperm was present at conception to produce a viable baby. A female's egg will only start to divide when it encounters the calcium spike produced by the presence of the male's sperm at fertilisation.

If the egg happens to experience a calcium spike without the presence of the male sperm it may begin to act as though it has been fertilised. Such a calcium spike cannot happen randomly though. In fertilisation it is a specific, targeted and precise change; it would not be possible to introduce a calcium spike by drinking milk! A defective sperm that lacks DNA might produce such a spike.

Under laboratory conditions, scientists have manipulated eggs to behave as though they are fertilised by injecting them with calcium.[99] Once fertilisation, or false fertilisation, has happened, the egg can complete the final stage of a cell division known as meiosis II, during which it loses half of its genetic material to make way for the genetic material of the sperm. If there is no sperm present, each half of the divided egg cell will die. In order for a virgin birth to carry on, the phantom-fertilised egg must not complete meiosis.

Both of these random factors, the calcium spike and the division mistake, could occur as the result of random dysfunctions or genetic defects. Assuming they do, the egg cell may then begin the process of

[99] I am not condoning such experimentation, just stating that it has happened.

parthenogenesis, or virginal development. Yet if this did occur, the result would not be a baby but a tumour made up of different kinds of tissue, liver, teeth, hair and so on. Parthenogenesis in humans never produces viable embryos because unfertilised eggs lack specific instructions about gene expression from the sperm.[100]

There's something else that I have not mentioned quite deliberately. If a spontaneous conception should occur, the resulting offspring would lack the genetic encoding of the male sperm, being deprived totally of the DNA of the mother. Any child would therefore be a girl. In fact, they would be a clone of the mother, identical to her in every way. The Balfour-Lynn study only asked for mothers of girls to come forward.[101]

Jesus did not lack the encoding of His Father. In reading some of the scientific discussions about the validity of Jesus' birth, they all assume that there is no father because Joseph is not involved. In today's world our minds leap to the idea that Joseph, or some other man, must have impregnated Mary because she gave birth to a boy. Our thinking is skewed by our societal standards, our own morality, our own unbelief. People struggle with the idea that there would even be a noble young woman who had kept herself for marriage. Virginity is sneered at by so many, yet it is so precious a gift that to save it for marriage, whether male or female, is a sign of purity of the highest order.

The Bible has never claimed that there was no father. It states that there was no *earthly* father. Its claim is that God is the Father of Jesus. The fact that we now know that a random, spontaneous conception would only produce a girl if it were ever successful shows that the miracle of the virgin birth is just that: a miracle. It cannot be explained or dismissed scientifically.

---

[100] Melinda Wenner Moyer; *Can a Virgin Give Birth?* http://www.slate.com/articles/news_and_politics/explainer/2007/12/can_a_virgin_give_birth.html, accessed 28/04/15.
This author is cited for her scientific knowledge only; I recognise that she does not support the idea of Jesus' virgin birth.

[101] R. Pianka; *Virgin Birth in Human Females?* http://www.zo.utexas.edu/courses/THOC/VirginBirth.html, accessed 28/04/15.

Liar, Liar?

The only other the possibility is that Mary lied. We know that she was not pregnant by Joseph for he sought to end the engagement.[102] He would not have sought to divorce if he were the father of the unborn child. He was a righteous man, a 'good bloke'. He wanted to do the right thing to save her reputation by ending things quietly. If he was the father, why not marry her? Why not expedite the wedding before she would show her pregnant state? The answer is that he was *not* the father. He had no desire to raise another man's child. He did not fully believe her either, for he heard her story and still decided to end their relationship.

Choose a Better Lie, Mary!

People lie all the time. Some studies claim that both men and women lie in approximately a fifth of their social exchanges lasting ten or more minutes; over the course of a week they deceive about thirty percent of those with whom they interact on a one-to-one basis.[103] That's a lot of lying going on at any one time. Intrinsically, because of our fallen nature, we all know how to lie. We like to differentiate these between white lies and life-and-death lies. White lies might be told to protect someone's feelings on the basis that what someone does not know will not hurt them. The truth though, when it does come to light, can cause such pain and mistrust between people that it is probably better to have been honest in the first place. Really big lies, where life is at risk, are told occasionally, but most people will never face this dilemma.

There is an example of this in the Bible, when the midwives lied to Pharaoh about the speed at which the Jewish slaves gave birth, in order to protect the lives of the children.[104] It appears that in some cases and on rare occasions a lie to protect life is justified. Casual lying is not acceptable to the Christian.[105]

---

[102] Matthew 1:19.

[103] Allison Kornet; www.psychologytoday.com/articles/199704/the-truth-about-lying, accessed 28/04/15. Published 01/05/97; reviewed 03/10/12.

[104] Exodus 1:19.

[105] Colossians 4:6.

The biggest lies are saved for those you are closest to, although lying between husband and wife is rare. Spouses lie to each other in 'only' about ten percent of their major conversations, but those tend to be the big betrayal lies.[106] Before you run off and accuse your husband, wife, boyfriend or girlfriend of some horrendous lie, remember that Christian relationships are built upon trust that flows from the love of God you have received. The issue is this: Mary's closest relationship is with Joseph and so was she lying to him?

Because everyone lies, everyone knows a real howler when they come across it. Without this becoming a training manual on how to lie, it is worth pausing and considering what makes a lie plausible. A good lie is short and to the point. It does not give too many details. People will judge whether the truth is being told by how much information is being given in answer to questions. Too much information will raise suspicions. This effect is called the 'falsifiability heuristic'. Secondly, a good lie is plausible. It answers the question in the mind of the other person: "How likely was that to have happened?" When you answer a question or give an excuse that seems farfetched people will assume you are lying. This phenomenon is called the 'infrequency heuristic'. People evaluate your responses by whether they seem likely or plausible. A good lie is hallmarked by calmness. People pay close attention to a person's level of nervousness. Stress leads people to question the validity of what is being said.[107]

Everyone Needs a Joseph[108]

The Bible does not give us an account of the conversation between Mary and Joseph. You can imagine it was quite a heated discussion. What Mary said was not believed by Joseph. He plans to save her

---

106 Allison Kornet; www.psychologytoday.com/articles/199704/the-truth-about-lying, accessed 28/04/15. Published 01/05/97; reviewed 03/10/12.

107 *How To Lie Effectively?* http://www.truthaboutdeception.com/lying-and-deception/howto-lie.html, accessed 28/04/15.
This secular website has much to say about the words we use to each other and this particular page is dedicated to how to lie to your partner without getting caught. I do not advocate its premise but merely cite it to illustrate the anatomy of lying.

108 Matthew 1:18-24.

reputation by putting aside their engagement quietly, but it can be deduced that he believes she is lying about who the father is for two reasons. Firstly, what she has told him has failed the plausibility test: "I'm pregnant with God's child; it's a boy and we are calling Him Jesus." This is all implausible.

God's child! This would have sounded crazy to him. Yes, they were all waiting for a Messiah and deliverer from Roman occupation, but surely that person would be from the upper strata of society.

A boy! How can you possibly know, Mary? There was no way of telling what gender a child would be in 1BC!

We're calling Him Jesus! You want to break with the family tradition of naming Him after me, even though he's not my child? Then everyone will know he is illegitimate.

The whole thing would have been nonsense to Joseph. Perhaps his reaction is why Mary later chose to store things in her heart when other miracles happened.[109]

Secondly, it's obvious Joseph did not believe her, for the angel had to tell him directly:

> *...an angel of the Lord appeared to him in a dream and said, "Joseph son of David, do not be afraid to take Mary home as your wife, because what is conceived in her is from the Holy Spirit. She will give birth to a son, and you are to give him the name Jesus, because he will save his people from their sins."*[110]

The news had been disturbing, destroying his world. He had always figured she was too good for him. Now he figured he was too good for her, and it hurt. A deep pain that would not easily be healed. He knew he was but a simple carpenter, but business was good and reliable and he knew he could provide. Maybe not the life she deserved – had *once* deserved – but an honest life filled with laughter and love. And children...

His mind wandered back to their conversation. "Joseph, I have something to tell you!" She had seemed so excited, yet peaceful, almost serene. If he did not know her better he would have thought

---

[109] Luke 2:19-52.

[110] Matthew 1:20-21.

she was resigned to her fate. This was different. She was – well – humble. "I have been visited by an angel. The Messiah is to come soon and I am to carry him. I'm pregnant with God's Son!" His world crumbled. They were from a small town, Nazareth, in Galilee, where everyone knew everyone else's business. You sneezed and a hundred people said bless you. You are expecting a child and by nightfall everyone knows. Everyone would know the child was not his. They would shame her. Her innocence and purity were two of the qualities that had attracted him to her in the first place.

He had tried to do everything right. People admired him for his ethics. Some called him righteous. The betrothal had been traditional. His parents had chosen the bride for him.[111] He was pleased with their choice and he knew they had seen his glances and admiring looks. They had asked her parents' consent first and then, with their agreement, Mary was asked.[112] The dowry was arranged and, like many, her parents chose a period of servitude. Not as long as Jacob's service to Laban, but enough for him to gift them with some new handmade furniture and fix a few things around the home.[113]

He had enjoyed spending time with her family; it gave him insight into their life and the kind of expectations Mary had of life. His love for her grew by the day. As was the norm, all communication between them had been via his best friend.[114] This was how things were done. It meant there could be no 'accidents', and Mary's virginity could be confirmed on the wedding night.

When she had sent word that she needed to talk, face to face with no one else around, he only agreed because it must have been very important for her to break with the conventions. He now realised she would have nothing left to lose. People would think what they would think anyway.

The village viewed them as married in many ways during this betrothal, so being unfaithful was punishable by death,[115] as it was for any marital unfaithfulness. His mind raced. He did not think they would stone her; the Romans frowned upon people taking the law,

---

111 Genesis 24, 21:21, 38:6.

112 Genesis 24:58.

113 Genesis 29; 1 Samuel 18:25.

114 John 3:29.

115 Deuteronomy 22:23-24.

even their own laws, into their own hands. She would be ostracised. Outcast. Alone. Better than death. She would have to go. Without him. Although not yet married, for he had not formally taken Mary into his own home, he could issue her a bill of divorce; he would do this quietly, without fuss.[116] There had been no blessing performed and no covenants had been entered into.[117] He could do this. Save face. Let her go with whomever the man she truly loved was.

He so wanted to believe her. He was waiting eagerly for the Messiah too. The whole nation was! Then the occupation and years of oppression from Rome would end. They could build a new kingdom under His reign. Surely He would come from noble blood. He knew he had a heritage, was part of the line of King David himself, but David had died twenty-eight generations ago and people did not think of Joseph as royalty.[118] He did not think of himself as royalty.

He slept fitfully that night. His night was permeated with thoughts and nightmares of her being shunned. Sometimes she was stoned. Other times mocked.

As the night lingered on his nightmares were interrupted with an inexplicable peace. His dream became filled with light. A man stood there in the middle of the light. Words gushed over Joseph as his soul was soothed. He knew this was more than just a dream. He knew this was real. He felt awake, alive, alert all at once. It was the angel Mary had spoken of.

It is all true! This is God's child. She has not been unfaithful! She loves me! She loves God too and is placing her life in His hands.

God is placing her life and that of Jesus, the Messiah, into Joseph's hands. Two vulnerable lives into the calloused hands of a carpenter. A Scripture bubbled to the surface of his mind, from Isaiah he was sure, that this was the fulfilment of prophecy: the virgin would conceive and give birth to a son and He would be God walking on earth.[119] With them. With everyone.

---

[116] Deuteronomy 24:1; Matthew 1:19.

[117] Ezekiel 16:8; Malachi 2:14; Proverbs 2:17; Genesis 24:60; Ruth 4:11-12. See note (iii) in 'Additional Notes' on page 240.

[118] Matthew 1:17.

[119] Isaiah 7:14.

He slept. Awaking the next morning he went to Mary's home, declared the betrothal at an end and took her to his own home.[120] They decided to keep themselves pure until after the birth of the baby. One day Mary would explain this to Matthew when he took such an interest in Joseph's genealogy. People would need to know that there was no possibility that Joseph was Jesus' biological father. He was a righteous man!

After this, Joseph knew she was not lying. He was to be a step-father to the Son of God. What seemed an improbable lie had now become the greatest privilege, a high calling and one he would take seriously. Joseph displays some incredible qualities.

Growing God's Plan

God's vision is always vulnerable in the early stages. Joseph has some big decisions to make before the call of God on his life is made clear.

Sometimes, when God is preparing you for a new thing, your life can seem to unravel. It is not that God has some plan to punish you, but sometimes for you to move forward He has to show you that change is inevitable. Many times things that began supernaturally end naturally. Elijah, during a drought that he had prophesied, went to the brook at Kerith as God commanded. He had everything he needed: water, food from birds, supernatural provision. Then after three years the brook dried up. The source had grown dry in the drought. The heavenly take out service stopped too. Then God spoke and said to go to the widow of Zarephath where he would be looked after. This was in the heart of Jezebel's power base, yet God would protect him.[121] It began supernaturally but ended naturally.

When God begins to shake things up around you, understand that He is orchestrating a change to place something else in your heart. Often that will be something that needs care, nurture and protection.

---

[120] Matthew 1:24-25. For many ordinary people this was the extent of a marriage ceremony once a period of service had been completed. Evidence of virginity would have been required. Normally the bed linen would be kept by the bride's mother for there would be signs of the hymen breaking during consummation. The Bible is clear that they remained celibate until after the birth of Jesus.

[121] 1 Kings 17:1-10ff.

Joseph was entrusted with the two most vulnerable people on the planet at that time: Mary, whose life needed protecting from the enemy's schemes – just think of the havoc if the enemy had discovered who she was and tried to end her life before Jesus was born! – and Jesus at this time was vulnerable too.

We know God warned Joseph when to move, where to go, where they would all be safe, but Joseph still had to get up and go![122] When God places a vision or a call in your life you have the responsibility to sustain it, cultivate it and grow it, for it will not survive without you!

Being Right or Being Righteous

Joseph was concerned with doing the right thing. The right thing was to protect Mary but to also issue a certificate of divorce. That would protect him too. His reputation would be intact. When people look to do the *right* thing it is often the thing that saves face for them, that keeps them in a good light, gives them an advantage. The *righteous* thing is different. Righteousness is sacrificial. It is doing the right thing even if your reputation is at risk or even lost. It is to do the right thing even when you are misunderstood or maligned. It is to do the right thing with graciousness and servanthood, even raising a child who is not yours, God's son. Many times in life you will have the opportunity to be right. Being right serves a sense of justice and ego. Being righteous is doing something higher than just being right; it is doing something for the greater good, for God's cause, for a bigger purpose. Something that outlives you. The last mention of Joseph is when Jesus is twelve years old, and then he is not mentioned by name.[123] Righteous people do not mind if they do not get the credit, are never thanked, or even if they do not see the fulfilment of what God has promised in their lifetime. They are not lofty or pious; they are grounded and rooted in their love for God. They are not zealous or bigots; they are loving and sacrificial. They are models. They are to be imitated to the extent they imitate Jesus.[124] You need

---

122 Matthew 2:13-18.
123 Luke 2:41-51.
124 1 Corinthians 4:16; 2 Thessalonians 3:9; Hebrews 6:12, 13:7; 3 John 1:11.

people like this in your life. People need you to be righteous examples to them.

Not a Lie, but True!

Is the virgin birth medically possible? No. Did it happen? Absolutely! That is why it is called a miracle!

The One who created your anatomy and the laws by which they operate is not subject to those laws Himself. He places within the egg of Mary the DNA and calcium required for Jesus to develop within the womb into a fully formed human being. He places in the heart of Mary and Joseph the faith they need to nurture and raise Jesus. He performs this miracle that can never be imitated and copied to set Jesus apart as unique. There will never be another virgin birth of a male child.

You need to have more confidence in this miracle. Christians over the years have become strangely muted on this subject; many do not hold that it occurred. Embarrassed by uncertainty, silence predominates. When I became a Christian I would regularly hear sermons on this subject. "No virgin birth, no Christianity," the preachers would say. It seems today's generation is not so sure that there was actually a virgin birth. There was. There has only ever been one. Your salvation depends upon it being so.

Mary Who?[125]

In some circles the young girl Mary is venerated, even worshipped, by those who see her devotion to God as holy. To others they minimise her role, fearful of worshipping anyone other than God.

Someone once explained to me their love for Mary, and the reason they prayed to her and not Jesus, as a simple belief that a Jewish mother will always nag her child to do what needed doing. I struggled with this and still do; there is only one mediator between us and God and that is Jesus.[126]

---

125 Luke 1:26-38.
126 1 Timothy 2:5.

There are attributes that we can, and should, learn from Mary though. Every Christian would benefit themselves and others if they displayed these.

FAITHFULNESS:

Mary had been brought up to believe that the Messiah was coming.

In the rabbinical traditions all children were educated in the Scriptures until a certain age. Then the boys would be separated from the girls and would learn more about the Scriptures. The best of the best of these were then separated again and trained further until the cream of the crop was identified and then, possibly, they would be assigned to a rabbi and would even progress to religious teacher themselves. Those boys who did not make the cut would learn the family business or trade. When Jesus astounded the religious teachers at the age of twelve there would probably have been offers to Joseph and Mary for Him to join a rabbinical school.[127] Wisely they refused. This is why the disciples' willingness to call Jesus 'Rabbi' is so poignant. They were not the best of the best yet were chosen by Jesus!

The development of a girl's life was somewhat different. At a young age, sometime before their teenage years and once they had gained a rudimentary knowledge of the Torah, they would continue developing the skills to be a good wife and run a household. This might sound an anathema to some of us but we need to understand that this was a patriarchal society. We also need to realise that Jesus did not operate in this way towards women. He treated them equally, taught them, appeared to them first and honoured them.[128]

Mary understood that there was to be a Messiah. She knew that this was to come through the miracle of a virgin birth.[129] She also knew that her own purity was something to be prized, not something to be given cheaply. Mary knew that she would be betrothed and that there would be the requirement for evidence of her virtue demanded by her future in-laws; otherwise any marriage would be null and void.

---

[127] Luke 2:41-52.

[128] Luke 10:41; John 20:11-18.

[129] Isaiah 7:14.

Faith for Mary was not displayed merely when the angel appeared to her. It was shown in her daily life, her faithfulness. She had kept herself pure. She was holy in the sense that she was wholly God's. Today lives are so full of things that pull people away from God. Mary's world may not have been as sophisticated and as technologically reliant as yours. Her life was simpler. She never allowed the simplicity of her life to leave her yearning for more. She was content. Pure. Innocent.

She invested in her real and present faith in God. Her awareness of the promised Messiah would not have been the first thought on her mind each day. Reality had to be dealt with, tasks completed, life had to be lived. Her life in fact had been pretty uneventful up until the point we read of her in Luke's Gospel. She had not stood out from the crowd and was already betrothed to Joseph. In fact, when Gabriel appeared to her and greeted her as "highly favoured one", she was troubled by the greeting.[130] Mary was faithful, but not spending each day thinking she would be the vessel for the Messiah. Her life was planned out. She was to marry the local carpenter and raise a family. She was content with this.

OBEDIENCE:

Faithfulness becomes an act of faith when greater obedience is called for. Mary's world is about to be turned upside-down. Everything she has planned in her mind is now in question as she hears God's plan for her life. Faithfulness has placed her in a position to be used of, for and by God for His greater purposes. Faithfulness has placed her on God's radar; she has gained His favour. Faithfulness means she can be trusted with more. The fate of the whole world will rest on her response.

Her mind runs through everything she has heard from Gabriel. Although she would have known about the promise of the Messiah and the requirements of the promise, she still asks, "How can this be, for I am a virgin?"

Mary did not, nor possibly did any of her the religious teachers, understand that when Isaiah proclaimed the virgin would give birth

---

130 Luke 1:29-30.

that this would be at God's instigation, not a natural union. She could not comprehend that she could be so used of God. *Me? Really!*

A prerequisite to obedience is asking questions. Do not think obedience must be blind to be complete. "Good soldiers are not allowed to question the intentions and orders of God..." – this is made to sound like it is a greater faith in some way. The truth is, to truly cooperate with God in His plans and mission, He loves our partnership and our questions. Not every question is a sign of doubt, but of cooperation.

I became a Christian through questioning. Those witnessing to me encouraged the questions, although I am not always sure that they had the answers to hand or that I was always completely satisfied with those answers. They were patient with me though. When I became a Christian, having questioned everything, I was then introduced to a church culture that seemed to deny the validity of asking questions, implying that God would not like us to question Him. This seemed bizarre to me – that I could ask questions before I was a Christian but once saved, I had to stop asking! I learn by asking questions!

When I was in training at Bible College I was placed in several churches. In the last placement I had requested to go to a large church in the area. This was not because I thought I was somehow special or worthy of this but because my previous placements had been in small churches – one of them I had co-led with another student – and I felt I had more to learn from experienced leaders. When I started this final year, David, the senior minister, said to me, "The best way to learn is to ask questions. Anything you want to know about why we do something the way we do, ask!" So I did.

At the end of the placement he commented, "I have been having Bible College students for fifteen years now, and you are the first one to ask me questions!" I learnt a lot from him, and our friendship endures to this day.

Sometimes God will ask things of us that will puzzle us. They should.[131] That does not mean that He refuses our questions or is displeased with them. He desires our cooperation even though He does not require it. Even grudging obedience is better than no

---

[131] Isaiah 55:8.

obedience. Be assured that conversing with God about what He is asking of you is not only alright, it is expected.[132] It is in the answers to the questions that the calling of God in your life is seared upon your spirit.

The most incredible words that leave Mary's mouth are found at the end of her conversation with the angel.

> *"I am the Lord's servant," Mary answered. "May your word to me be fulfilled."*[133]

This is often quoted as a proof text of obedience, forgetting her fear and puzzlement that led to this statement. Mary had reached a point where she was willing to risk everything in this act of obedience. It was not reckless obedience, but well considered and thought through. She was going to have to talk with Joseph. She would probably have to call off the wedding, leave town, be alone for the rest of her life. She did not know. She did know she was chosen – unexpectedly, suddenly and surprisingly.

There were more spiritual girls than her in Israel. There were more worthy ones. There were more beautiful ones. She had everything to lose, nothing to gain. Despite impossible odds, ridicule and potential ostracising, Mary said yes!

Mind the Gap!

Willingness is part of obedience, but willingness is more to do with a battle with fear. Fear has to be overcome first before obedience can be displayed; willingness is the key. It is an act of the will to be willing. It is a decision to move forward. I have heard it said so many times from pulpits that God does not need talent, He just needs us to be willing. That's true to a degree. God can invest us with gifts and talents as He wills; where we lack something we can even learn a new skill too.

Willingness, though, is not passively waiting for something to happen. I will say it again; willingness is an act of the will! Decide to cooperate with the plans of God. Mary did not just say yes; she

---

132 Amos 3:7.

133 Matthew 21:28-31.

submitted her will to God's plan: "Let it happen to me just as you have said!"

There is always a gap between where you are and where God calls you to be. A prophecy may be received, or a Scripture, or you may respond to a sermon or reading a book, and then that call of God in your life surfaces. There is always a gap though between the 'now' and the 'then' of that promise. I have lost count of the number of times I have had the following kind of conversations:

"Pastor, I believe the Lord has called me to the missions field to China!"

"That's great! What a wonderful thing God has called you to do! So what are you doing about it?"

"Well, I'm praying about it. And I have googled China. I'm just waiting for God to say, 'Go!'"

"OK, but what *else* are you doing?"

"Well, I am willing to go when He is ready to send me."

It is normally around this point that I will say something like, "How are the Mandarin lessons going?"

"Mandarin?"

"Sure, Mandarin. If you're called there and if you are willing to go, surely you'll be gaining the skills to be able to minister in some way. You need some basic language skills. You might even need a qualification, like nursing or something in agriculture, so that the government there will welcome you into their country. God is obviously willing to send you, for as you have said, He has called you there. What are you actually doing to show you are willing to go?"

For 'China', feel free to insert whatever territory or task you feel called to. People will often say that they are willing but do nothing to show that their will has bowed to the Lord. Willingness is a battle with fear. As much as they say they are willing, they might be fearful of failure. There is no guarantee that the mission anyone is called to will be a success. Sometimes the job is to scatter seed or to water it, but ultimately, it is God who causes things to grow and succeed.[134]

You do not know where you will fit in the plan that God has. You are a co-worker, getting your own reward, and therefore successful in God's sight. To those around you, you may have failed

---

[134] 1 Corinthians 3:5-9.

in the task. What of the person who feels called to our metaphorical missions field? Suppose they do all they can to narrow the gap between where they are and where they are to go. Suppose they do go and after many years they have no converts. They return in old age and retire to some generic home for the elderly, seeing out their last days in anonymity. Have they failed? Perhaps years after they leave another missionary enters the village where decades before a servant of God prayer-walked the dusty streets saturating the place with intercessions, breaking up the fallow ground. This new missionary begins to see many converts, a clinic open and a new school. They get plaudits; finances roll in from the Western Church as news of their achievements reach the churches who can resource them. Who is the most successful of the two who answered the call? I would suggest the greater reward in heaven would go to the first one who answered the call but saw no immediate fruit! That does not work in our fleshly minds; in God's thinking it makes perfect sense.

Obedience says, "I will do it." Willingness walks the journey.

Everyone Needs an Elizabeth![135]

Joseph has married Mary but there is still much to be assimilated, thought through and processed. The angel also told her about her cousin Elizabeth, pregnant at an old age, a miracle. It is not surprising that Mary was unaware of this news. Families did not travel outside of their village or town often. Mary knows that she is the only one carrying the Messiah – there were never going to be two – but she rushes to Elizabeth, her older cousin, as soon as possible, in her first trimester. She needs to be around someone who understands that miracles happen, especially miracles around the birth of children. As she arrives and greets her cousin, Elizabeth's baby, John the Baptist, leaps at the sound of her voice.[136]

Babies move in the womb. Our three sons all seemed to be trying out for the England rugby team from when they could move in Barbie's womb. This was particularly uncomfortable for her from the sixth month onwards as the baby made more and more room for himself.

---

[135] Luke 1:5-45.
[136] Luke 1:41.

For Elizabeth this is more than the moving of her son. She knows the difference. The Holy Spirit fills her and she declares God's goodness over Mary, before Mary has said that she too is pregnant.[137] When God is moving in your life, be it miraculously, through circumstances, through relationships, through prophecy or any other way, it can be bewildering, even confusing at times. It does matter how you respond, in faith and confidence that God is in control. It is also important that you go and seek out those who have walked the road ahead of you.

Who You Gonna Call?

When God speaks to you and you feel a call of God, you need to share this carefully, prudently, and wisely. Not everyone is going to celebrate with you the call on your life. Most won't. It's not that Christians are bad people or deliberately discouraging. They are people though and people do not always say the right thing. In the turmoil of what was happening with Mary, God knew that she would need someone who understood. Someone who was experiencing her own miracle. Someone a little farther down the road than Mary. Someone called Elizabeth.

No calling is going to equal that of Mary's – she birthed the Messiah, after all – but whatever you feel called to do, it will seem momentous and beyond you. There is an exhilaration that comes and you will want to tell the world. That would have been dangerous for Mary and the baby in the womb. She may have faced death. Herod tried to kill Jesus later on.[138] Like Mary carrying Jesus, your calling needs nurturing. So who do you tell?

Look for some of these qualities:

SHARED PRAISE:

Elizabeth praises with Mary. She blesses her. She is excited for her and with her, even though she may not fully understand Mary's situation. Elizabeth blesses Mary; she cherishes her young cousin enough to love her through and in her calling. This releases praise

---

[137] Luke 1:42-45.

[138] Matthew 2:16.

and worship in Mary.[139] We often think this song of praise was immediately sung after Gabriel appeared. It wasn't. It would not have been a safe environment for Mary to give public praise in Nazareth. She was now married to Joseph, but had travelled to Elizabeth. Gabriel had told Mary of this other pregnancy, remember? They share their joy with each other and they share praise to the Father together.

SHARED EXPERIENCES:

When sharing your call get alongside someone farther in the journey than you. Look for someone who has a similar call and go and pick their brains.

Elizabeth has also had an extraordinary experience. Her husband is mute! She has a name for her child that breaks family tradition. Gabriel appeared to Zachariah and announced her pregnancy too. Elizabeth had been unable to conceive and was beyond the age of child bearing.[140] She would understand the anguish and perplexing nature of a supernatural encounter but she has also lived through the commotion of her husband, a priest, having to scribble what happened before the altar to his fellow priests for he could not talk. She knows what it was like to be called to fetch him and have to care for him through his frustrations. Elizabeth also knows what it is like to carry a child; she can coach Mary through the early stages of her pregnancy.

Look for someone farther down the road than you and learn from them.

SHARED VALUES:

A little-quoted verse in this account is:

> *Mary stayed with Elizabeth for about three months and then returned home.*[141]

Why is this significant? We know that Elizabeth is already six months along in her pregnancy when Mary arrives.[142] She then stays

[139] Luke 1:46-55.
[140] Luke 1:5-25.
[141] Luke 1:56.

three months. In the culture of the day Mary would have been serving her older relative. They have shared values; they are both carrying promises of God.

There is still a definite relationship of honour and servitude though. Mary served her cousin. It is possible, given the timeframe, that Mary acted as a midwife for Elizabeth too. It is unlikely that she would have left a few days before the baby was born. Even when you feel you have a call, even if that calling is greater than your mentor's in your eyes, serve them. Callings are not released in the Kingdom of God through plotting, ambition, or selfish gain, but through serving the needs of those around us.

Share it with Leaders

You need to share your calling with your leaders. Too often people do not. For some this is an aversion to the shadow of the abuses of the 'heavy shepherding movement', which has nothing to do with overweight pastors, but a wing of the Charismatic church overstepping biblical authority. Even if you became a Christian after this happened, the culture of church you experience will have been affected by it. The error was that leaders involved themselves in every decision people would make and, although sincere, for many this became intolerable. The leaders involved have long since repented and such abuses should not occur today. This has left the Church with a scar though, a shadow of mistrust about telling leaders and pastors about things in their heart, even if a particular fellowship has never shown any heavy shepherding traits. Do not forget that your leaders are there to care for you, guide you, guard you from folly and to help you develop into the best that you can be. It is their role to prepare you and to guide you into works of service.[143] Good leaders will set you on course to closing the gap between your calling and your commissioning.

The New Testament model for being commissioned is not to shake your feet of the dust of the church, but to send you at the right time.[144] If you approach your leaders with humility and openness they

---

[142] Luke 1:36.

[143] Hebrews 13:7,17; Ephesians 4:11-13.

[144] Compare Luke 10:8-12 with Acts 13:2.

will love to pray with you, seek God with you and train you for greater things.

Every good leader's heart is that their ceiling would be your floor! When I was called to ministry in the sense of church leadership the first person I told was my pastor at that time, John Harrison. He was great and so encouraging. I was only thirteen-and-a-half, but he knew what to do. He prayed with me, told me what to read, how to pray, how to read the Bible, how to serve. To supplement his income he ran paper delivery rounds for a weekly paper. He put me to work on one of his paper rounds, teaching me in my early teens I had to show up to work. He modelled this for me. At one point he shared my calling with the church (with my permission). He took me to youth camps and had me digging cesspits and putting up tents before the campers arrived. He taught me how to serve. He put me in the church's first home group (revolutionary in the early 1980s), and encouraged me to lead Bible studies at the age of fourteen. He appointed me, under our youth leader, to the youth committee at fifteen and had me preaching by the time I was sixteen, having shown I could handle the Word of Truth in smaller ways, and blessed me as I preached elsewhere soon after. He is as much responsible for my ministry today as I am.

When he left the church to take up another pastorate my second mentor and friend-to-be took over, Billy Fenning. Billy saw all the same potential but also saw that underneath was an arrogance to me too. He would not allow me to preach and so after a few years I left to work with a Christian group as a youth evangelist. I did not leave well. There was no overt confrontation, but in my heart I was not right. After eight years, having lived overseas, married, become a father of two sons at the time, and having some of my kinks ironed out, I was back in Billy's office apologising for my arrogance. I promised him I would not do anything unless he released me. I cleaned the toilets, drove the minibus and over time Billy could see I placed a higher value on service than my ego or position. He let me lead a home group. He let me preach. It was he who suggested I apply for a ministerial credential with our movement. It was he who blessed me, released me to Bible College and supported my family there for three years. It was he who invited me to share a platform with him in Africa training other leaders on more than one occasion. I owe much to these two men of God and others along the way who have identified and nurtured the call of God in my life.

If you feel called then submit that calling to friends, but it will be those in leadership who will nurture you to fruitfulness. Sow servitude into your ministry, as Mary did, and you will reap the reward for that in time. You will also discover that in time others will come to you to sow into their lives too. It is a cyclical process in which lone rangers and mavericks learn cooperation, Kingdom thinking and service. It's an adventure!

CHAPTER TWELVE

Temptations of Jesus

The Bible is clear: evil behaviour separated everyone from God. There is no grey area here. Sin separates you from God.

Today behaviours are not punished, corrected or guided in the same way they were a generation ago. In the generation before mine it would be enough for the policeman to reprimand a pre-teen verbally for the child to never recommit the offence. In the generation before that, it was not uncommon in the UK for a policeman to give a child a 'clip around the ear'.

Before you think that I am wanting those days to return, I am not. It does illustrate though that behaviour has been redefined in society. Sin simply does not exist in the mindset of the young – or the old, for that matter. Previously you would have seen what may have been called 'teenage rebellion'; today there is little to rebel against as societal pressures and political correctness continue to take their course. There is no such thing as rebellion any longer for any age group, just behaviour.

Intuitively you know that this is wrong. You know that not all conduct is right. This intuition does not find its meaning in the decay of morality, the tensions in our communities, or the waywardness of young or old; it is rooted in the separation sin brings to lives. The aloneness. The God-absentness. It is not that God has separated Himself from you, but isolation and insulation exist.[145]

[145] Colossians 1:21-22; 1 John 2:16 (NKJV); Matthew 4:1-11.

The way you live your life may not seem at all bad to you. People are great at comparing themselves with others and how they live, and whilst not saintly, you are not as bad as some people.

That only works in God's sight if your neighbours and friends are the standard by which you gain access to a relationship with Father God. They are not; Jesus is. He is the only man to have lived and never been separated, alienated or dispatched from the presence of God for His behaviour. At the cross He was forsaken by God, alone, not because of His lifestyle but because of humankind's!

Alone in the Wilderness

When experiencing your wilderness times, the tendency is to equate those experiences with abandonment. They are not easy times. They can come in an instant, sometimes expressed in a personal tragedy, a redundancy, or children rebelling against God. Sometimes they can seem to come for no reason at all. Everything seems the same as it did yesterday, the sun's still shining, the disciplines of Christian life are still being practised, yet something just feels a little off in your spirit. You feel alone. You are not. This is why it is called the Christian faith, not the Christian feelings.

Jesus is led into the wilderness by the Spirit.[146] Luke's retelling says that Jesus was full of the Spirit and was led to the wilderness and later returned in the power of the Spirit.[147] You can be left with the idea that the Spirit bookends the wilderness experience; He takes Jesus in and waits for Him to return. This makes the Holy Spirit seem more like an obedient Labrador than part of the Godhead. No, the Spirit *went with Jesus*. It is the role of the *paraklete*, the Greek word for the Spirit, to be the Counsellor. Jesus had been filled with the Spirit; Luke makes this clear too.

The wilderness is a tough place. It is a place where prayers are harder to pray and answers seem harder to hear. It is a place where you can feel downcast. It is not a place of abandonment. It is not a place of isolation. The Spirit went with Jesus. In tough times He is still with you. Listen to Paul's words about tough times:

---

146 Matthew 4:1.
147 Luke 4:1-14.

> *But we have this treasure in jars of clay to show that this all-surpassing power is from God and not from us. We are hard pressed on every side, but* <u>*not*</u> *crushed; perplexed, but* <u>*not*</u> *in despair; persecuted, but* <u>*not*</u> *abandoned; struck down, but* <u>*not*</u> *destroyed. We always carry around in our body the death of Jesus, so that the life of Jesus may also be revealed in our body. For we who are alive are always being given over to death for Jesus' sake, so that his life may be revealed in our mortal body.*[148]

The place may be arid but your spirit does not have to be dry! The wilderness is not a destination, but it is certainly part of the journey. It is something that is passed through.

Read again the age-old wisdom of the words of one of the most beloved passages of Scripture, Psalm 23. This Psalm is loved. I want the restoration of my soul. I want the still waters. I sometimes want those who have wronged me to be serving my dinner one day! Not so keen on the valley of the shadow of death! That sounds creepy. It tends to be read at funerals. The promise is not for when death comes, but for whilst you live. The shadow of something is not the actual thing itself. It does speak of a total darkness though where light is blocked and vision is diminished.

The emphasis of the verse is walking *through* the valley of the shadow of death, not camping there, not making it your destination. I guess that is an option and, sadly, some tend to get stuck in their Christian life. If that is you, as you read these words, can I lovingly implore you to get up and continue your Christian walk? The Christian walk is about movement. Keep going. Do not give up. Your sunrise is coming.

In the midst of the wilderness you are told that the Shepherd's rod and staff comfort you. The rod was used by the shepherd to ward off predators, to give them a good *thwack!* Even in the darkness Jesus is defending you from evil. The rod symbolises the shepherd's authority over that which attacks the sheep, especially in darkness. The staff speaks of the love and tenderness the shepherd has for the sheep. It has a crook at one end that the shepherd will have shaped and sanded until smooth so it would not hurt the flock. He guides the sheep with

---

148 2 Corinthians 4:7-11, emphasis mine.

it, lifts them out of danger when they are trapped and even uses it to lift a newborn lamb to its mother so that she does not reject her offspring, for if he touched it, it would carry the scent of a man. The rod and the staff of the Good Shepherd protect you and guide you, bringing comfort in the wilderness.

Jesus shows you what the wilderness can be like and what it is meant to be like. It is never easy. Jesus was tempted in every way you are but did not sin.[149] Do not think that this is not possible, that the pressures on this generation are far more than in Christ's generation. Sin is the same as it has always been. It is primarily a heart issue. Then it is a mind issue. Then it is an action. Something is craved, thought about, acted out. People desire something and then dwell on that thing mentally until succumbing. In one sense temptation works the same way as a godly desire: you crave it, think it, do it.

Immediately after Jesus' baptism we would expect Him to go straight into ministry, healing the sick, raising the dead, performing miracles. He did not. He spent forty days and nights contending with the enemy. Was this necessary? Surely the cross would have been enough? The cross is more than enough and His blood complete for the forgiveness of your sins. There is a journey to the cross that began at His baptism. It included healing the sick, confounding the religious with His teaching, realigning the expectations of the disciples as to what the Kingdom would look like, demonstrating what relationship with God should be like and more. The journey to the cross also included another reality: the devil needed to be defeated by a man where Adam had failed.

The Bible tells us that there are three areas of sin. There are subcategories to each of these, but generally speaking there are three spheres where the enemy of your soul tries to gain an unholy advantage. These are what the Bible calls "the lust of the flesh", "the lust of the eyes" and "the pride of life".[150] Jesus was tempted in each of these areas in the wilderness.

---

149 Hebrews 4:15 Hebrews 4:15.

150 1 John 2:16 (NKJV).

More Than a Bit Tired

The Bible is understated about Jesus' physical condition after forty days and nights fasting; it simply says He was hungry![151] Most would be hungry after a day's fast. The truth is in the West true hunger is not known. After forty days and nights Jesus was at His lowest physical ebb. The enemy came at this point, when Jesus was most susceptible to his suggestion, so he thought. That is his technique, to wear you down and attack at a low point, building footholds in your life. The same action is repeated over and over; a foothold becomes a stronghold. If Jesus would fall in any area, just once, the devil would keep coming back to the same area continually.

Temptation 1: Look Inward

The tempter came to Him and said, "If you are the Son of God, tell these stones to become bread." [152]

At this point in Jesus' wilderness nothing could have been more appetising than hot, fresh bread. There is nothing like warm bread and butter! You may even be salivating right now.

This is what the Bible calls the lust of the flesh. These are sins that satisfy some kind of physical desire. Hunger, thirst, sex... Even exercise can become addictive as the body craves the endorphin highs that come as a result.

The enemy is hitting Jesus at the most obvious point of weakness. He is not appealing to Scripture here; he doesn't need to. "You're hungry, Jesus, very hungry, physically weak; some bread would help. If you're who you say you are, a little miracle to serve yourself won't hurt." It sounds reasonable. Temptation always does when weighed against your desires. It's a craving that will only be satisfied by one thing; so it seems in that moment.

Jesus uses the Scriptures to overcome the temptation.

It is written: "Man does not live on bread alone, but on every word that comes from the mouth of God."[153]

---

151 Matthew 4:2.
152 Matthew 4:3.
153 Matthew 4:4.

There is a key here, one that repeats throughout this encounter, that the written Scripture has power. Jesus did not say it would be wrong, but there was something better. Imagine what kind of Saviour He would be if the miracles He performed were self-serving rather than a response to Father's will and compassion? He would not be the Saviour at all; at best a magician in the enemy's court! The Scriptures do not say bread is bad, nor that satisfying genuine hunger is bad either, but that there is something better: the words from the mouth of God. These can sustain you beyond your physical desires, beyond your weak willpower, to a place of communing with Father God.

Jesus alluded to this later in His ministry when the disciples thought that someone else had brought Him food. Jesus said He had food they did not know about, to do the will of Father who had sent Him.[154] How did Jesus know what His Father's will was? He listened to what Father was saying. Something He would not have been able to do again had He turned stones into bread!

Jesus succeeded here so you can hear the voice of God too, for He has made a way for you to enter into a relationship with Him. That's why the Bible on the bedside table is so powerful. Your opinion may tell you it's okay to give into this type of sin. *God understands, right? He made me!* Our thoughts are weak and influenced by ungodly desires. The Word is written so that you know a framework of right and wrong that comes from outside of the self, that your morality is not subjective, depending on *your* thoughts, but objective, depending on *God's* thoughts. Seeing the better way before us in Scripture takes us into a deeper relationship with Father.

Temptation 2: Look at Me!

There is a craving in the human psyche for attention. This is rooted in every person's need for love. If this is not satisfied properly in the early, formative years of a person's life, then there can be a tendency to either become unnaturally introverted, shunning relationships and human interactions, or overly self-centric, promoting one's own actions and achievements beyond their actual

---

[154] John 4:31-34.

value. It's the "look at me" attitude that is simply attention-seeking. The Bible calls this the pride of life.

Satan's plan is to have you so ego-centred, so selfish in your motivations, that you do not see the needs of others around you any longer. This was the root of this temptation that Jesus faced:

> *"If you are the Son of God," he said, "throw yourself down. For it is written: 'He will command his angels concerning you, and they will lift you up in their hands, so that you will not strike your foot against a stone.'"* [155]

Think about how impressive that would have looked. Think about what a contrast that was to the baby being born and laid in a manger some thirty years earlier. Surely this would have been a more appropriate entrance for the Saviour of the world! *Look at me!* The worship of Jesus cannot be a bad thing, right?

The trap that Satan is setting for Jesus is the one where he himself fell. He has tried and failed to have Jesus fall by looking at His own needs. Now He is trying to have Jesus fall as he, the devil, fell. The pride of life does not actually get anyone to look at you or me in a healthy way; it's pitiful and limiting, a dead end.

The devil is quoting Scripture here.[156] He knows the Bible too. Sadly, he knows it better than many who profess Christ as their Lord and Saviour. I find it interesting that Jesus does not tell the enemy that he is misquoting the Psalms. He points to a greater principle: do not test God.

> *Jesus answered him, "It is also written: 'Do not put the Lord your God to the test.'"* [157]

God *can* intervene if Jesus throws Himself down, but the Kingdom of God was to be built upon service and the invitation to accept Jesus, the servant King. It was not going to be built upon a spectacular demonstration that would draw attention artificially to Jesus and lead to a kingdom that was dictatorial in nature.

When the enemy misquotes the Bible to fool you and tempt you, look for the higher Kingdom principle. This will also be embedded in

---

155 Matthew 4:6.
156 Psalm 91:11-12.
157 Matthew 4:7.

Scripture but it will always have the hallmark of love and serving others rather than deliberately drawing attention to you. The answer to, "Look at me!" is always going to be, "Look at Him!" Paul puts it this way:

And you should imitate me, just as I imitate Christ.[158]

Temptation 3: Look at That!

The last temptation for Jesus at this time was a 'lust of the eyes' type of encounter.

"All this I will give you," he said, "if you will bow down and worship me." [159]

The worship part of this temptation is almost whispered. It's not the thing he wants Jesus to actually focus on, after all; that would be obviously wrong! The enemy does not headline the obvious, but the tempting! "All this I will give to you..." is when the devil shows Jesus the world and its kingdoms. The lust of the eyes is that which can be seen, that which can be taken, circumventing the processes of God.

This is a temptation that Adam and Eve fell for:

When the woman saw that the fruit of the tree was good for food and pleasing to the eye, and also desirable for gaining wisdom, she took some and ate it. She also gave some to her husband, who was with her, and he ate it.[160]

It looked good! Lots of things look good. Looking for easy ways to accomplish goals – from shortcuts to success, to get-it-quick answers – is a big temptation. If Jesus had dwelt upon what He was being shown it may have looked good to Him too, but He did not! Thank God!

Jesus in the wilderness had everything Adam did in the garden! Adam had the presence of God; Jesus had the Spirit. Adam had the uninterrupted presence of God until the Fall where he hid from God; Jesus did not hide Himself from God in the wilderness. Adam had a lush place to inhabit; Jesus had an arid place. Adam had everything

---

158 1 Corinthians 4:16.
159 Matthew 4:10.
160 Genesis 3:6.

he needed and more; Jesus had to reclaim the rights to the Eden experiences as a man. He did this by relying on the presence of the Spirit and the Word of God. As a sun-parched, weather-beaten, food-and-sleep-deprived man, Jesus had to stand in the place Adam found himself, outside of paradise. He overcame to open up a new paradise for you, a new life of fullness and abundance, and eventually heaven.

The temptation Jesus is being shown is a hollow victory, a mirage of paradise, a faux reality, a cheap facsimile of what could be. He is being shown what He would win at the cross, His inheritance. If He succumbs He'll actually receive nothing. The enemy does the same with you. You may have a vision of what could be and what you can achieve in life and then he comes to offer you an early inheritance. This always leads to problems. Proverbs tells us:

> *An inheritance quickly gained at the beginning will not be blessed at the end.*[161]

Trying to circumvent the processes of God is like trying to reach a destination with no directions or satnav; it is aimless. Christians will often be event-focussed, tending to live for the moment when the walls of a Jericho will come tumbling down, the moments of victory and breakthrough. They do not tend to celebrate the trudging round those walls every day for six days and then, on victory day, marching around them another seven times.[162] When the children of Israel walked around the city on the first day there was not much reward, but they had created a path. When hundreds of thousands of people walked around Jericho for one day they crushed any vegetation and left a mark. Understand this: when you are walking around your Jericho you always leave a mark. Something begins to change in the topography of the land even if you do not feel it.

After six days this new pathway around Jericho would have been so downtrodden that it may have begun to feel like a rut. Doing the same thing over and over and over again can seem pointless. On the seventh day the people may have groaned a little, for they now had to walk around Jericho another seven times. Their faith may have wavered, their desire to overcome may have waned, but they just kept

---

[161] Proverbs 20:21.

[162] Joshua 6:1-21.

walking. Grudging obedience is better than no obedience. Last time around, and maybe they did not know it was actually the last time, but Joshua knew. The trumpets sounded and they all had to shout, loudly, victoriously.

Having walked around their wall thirteen times and only seen a rut created, it may have been hard to shout, but shout they did. Then there was a rumbling sound, a cracking, dust rising from the inside of the walls in response to the vibrations and – *crash!* – down they came. The battle was over before it had begun. The city was routed and dedicated to God.

Victory!

The event, the moment, the breakthrough! That is the thing about breakthrough moments; there has to be something to be broken through! God delivers you in the moment but you also have to celebrate the processes too. Celebrate the new pathways that are created. Be simple in obedience and simply obedient. The trumpet will sound over your situation. Even if it does not, there is another trumpet that will sound one day soon, and heaven will open up and Jesus will return.[163] Either way your victory is assured!

When the devil says to Jesus, "All this I will give you," he is saying, "There's another way. You don't need to trudge around here on earth. You don't need the hassle or the frustration. It's a shortcut to the same result." It never is and the result is never the same. Besides anything, Satan underestimated how much pleasure Jesus would get from simply being with people, walking with them, healing them, giving hope to the hopeless and life to the lifeless.

The shortcuts in life will always be reflected in the object of worship. That was the caveat. All this could be Jesus' if He would bow and worship Satan. The devil did not need to even say this. If Jesus had succumbed and accepted the devil's deal, it would have been a de facto act of worship. It would have been taking the trust that Jesus had placed in Father God to raise Him from the dead after three days and circumventing this by placing His trust in the devil. You trust whom you worship and worship whom you trust. God should consume you as your passion and sole purpose.

---

[163] 1 Thessalonians 4:16-18.

Jesus' sole passion was to do the will of the One who had sent Him.[164] Satan's sole passion has always been the worship of himself instead of God. This is the very reason he was cast out from heaven in the first place. Created with brilliance and splendour, music and the ability to lead within his very being, Lucifer was the angel of light. The glory he had, the worship he expressed, was all a reflection of the majesty of God. He was designed to a be a signpost to the Holy One. Instead he craved that glory for himself.[165] It has always been his goal to be worshipped. This can be subtle and does not mean that people have to become full time Satan-worshippers in some cult. It happens when you place anything above the priority of worshipping God in your life. The Bible calls that idolatry. The devil calls that victory. Jesus calls that split loyalty.[166]

Jesus' response is quick, passionate and direct:

> *"Away from me, Satan! For it is written: 'Worship the Lord your God, and serve him only.'"*

Note that Jesus does not *request* Satan leave, but *commands* him to. He is not intimidated because of where His worship is directed. He has a confidence about Him that comes from being filled with the Spirit and being constantly in the presence of God through worship. He does not need to be side-tracked and does not even entertain the shortcut. His mind and heart are fixed upon the purposes of God.

If the enemy can take your eyes off of God and place them on a perceived shortcut, he has already won. The Bible instructs us to fix our eyes on Jesus. Look in one place. Focus! Do not get distracted by what you think looks good to you.[167] Everything you need for your trumpet sound of victory is unlocked through the worship of God.

Not Over Yet!

There is a strange idea that Jesus was only tempted on three occasions during a forty-day period at the beginning of His ministry.

---

164 John 6:38.

165 Ezekiel 28:12-19; Isaiah 14:13-14. Both these passages use poetic language to describe the fall of Satan.

166 Luke 16:13.

167 Hebrews 12:2.

Matthew simply says the devil then left Jesus and that angels came and tended to Him. Matthew gives the impression that the devil simply gave up. For his Jewish readers this would have been amazing, for many believed that the demonic inhabited arid places. Jesus mentions this belief when warning about those who are set free only to reject Christ and end up in a worse state than before.[168] For Matthew's audience, the fact that Jesus gains victory in the desert is a sign of His complete divinity.

Luke seems more pragmatic:

> *When the devil had finished all this tempting, he left him until an opportune time.*[169]

Luke is not denying the victory of Jesus in the wilderness. He is saying what you know to be true: the enemy is persistent. The Bible does not specifically say that Jesus endured any more temptations; the devil looked for opportunities to try again. Remember that the Bible tells us that Jesus was tempted in every way you are and yet did not sin.[170] All temptations have the same three roots; the devil is persistent but he is low in variety. So, for example, Jesus was tempted with the lust of the flesh to turn stones to bread, but He would have also been tempted sexually, or with any manner of things, yet did not sin. Being tempted is not a sin. That's part of being human. Flirting with and giving into temptation is sin.

The enemy will always look for more opportune times in your life to make you fall. Once he has established a pattern in life it becomes harder and harder to overcome the sins that so easily grab you. Be on guard. The devil still tries to imitate Jesus by prowling like a roaring lion.[171] The Bible does not say that he is a lion, but he is trying to intimidate like one, poorly imitating the majesty of the Lion of the Tribe of Judah.[172]

In Mel Gibson's film *The Passion of the Christ,* Gibson captures something of this in the portrayal of the enemy at the flogging of Christ. This ghostly figure, sinister and intimidating, walks through

---

[168] Matthew 12:43-45.
[169] Luke 4:13.
[170] Hebrews 4:15.
[171] 1 Peter 5:8-9.
[172] Revelation 5:5.

the crowd quizzically looking at Jesus. There is something tangible about that scene. A prowling enemy. He parades around looking for his next meal. Make sure you're not on his menu! As a believer you will always be on his wish list, but do not offer yourself as the main course for his dinner!

The problem is people think of temptation and sin differently to Jesus! Being tempted is not a sin. Giving into that temptation is a sin. Entertaining that temptation is sinful; that is, allowing a foothold to develop in the mind that will eventually fracture and allow all manner of behaviours to become normal in life.

How many times have you said, "I will never do such and such," only one day to replace that sentiment with, "I never intended to get into this mess."? Look away from the 'lust of the eye' temptation. Jesus did not dwell on what was before Him. In fact, He quickly aligned His focus on God.

There's Hope for Us All

The great news is that Jesus' victory in the desert means you can throw yourself upon the lavish love and grace of God. When failure comes you are not left alone in these wilderness experiences.

God always provides a way out.[173] Sometimes the silliest prayers in tempting situations are uttered, such as, "Lord, if you don't want me to do this bad thing then close the door." This is just denying that there is a free will. These things are choices; as much as the devil tempts you, the choice is always yours whether to continue on a wrong path or not. Often the way out God provides is simply the same as the one He provided for Joseph when in the clutches of Potiphar's wife: run![174]

Turn back to God. Allow His love to overwhelm you and His forgiveness to restore you.

---

[173] 1 Corinthians 10:13.
[174] Genesis 39:11-12.

CHAPTER THIRTEEN

Jesus' Vulnerability

Fear and anxiety are human traits. There are things that happen in life that can bring an inner turmoil that no one else would understand from the perspective of the sufferer.

When I was a young, about eight years old, I was mauled by a white Alsatian dog; it was bigger than me and left wounds the length of my right leg, exposing the bone. After a visit to the hospital I was discharged and placed under the care of the GP. In those days they would visit convalescing patients at home. On his first visit he discovered some puncture wounds that were missed at the hospital, which wasn't surprising given the state of my leg. I can remember being bandaged from my ankle to my groin and under strict instructions not to walk for six weeks. Recuperative care has changed somewhat since the 1970s, but this meant my stepfather ended up carrying me everywhere. It was the summer holidays, so there was no playing outside for me. It was not the best of times!

This led to a chronic fear of dogs. I am not talking about a dislike of them but full blown panic attacks if I saw one within a hundred metres. If I heard one barking in a house I would cross the road in case it managed to break out and chase me in the street. This may sound irrational, but in my mind, this could happen. As I grew I tried all I could do to avoid these pesky canine menaces. In my teen years I had friends who had dogs. I learnt to control my fear to a degree and would be fine around smaller dogs if the owner was present, but the bark of a dog would still bring out a cold sweat.

Years later I was engaged to be married to my lovely wife and life was good. I had learnt to manage my fear by just not being around dogs. That tends to be the way people deal with fear or a wound in their lives: avoid it. Life can be lived that way but it is still life that is limited. One day Barbie was on her way to visit and I had popped out to get some milk. Walking back towards my flat I rounded the corner and a dog ran out of the very first apartment and stood between me and my destination, barking ferociously in some kind of possessed frenzy. I stopped dead. I couldn't move. My heart was racing. I was just thinking, "Don't bite me! Don't bite me!"

Barbie had arrived and was waiting in her car for me to let her in. She saw what was happening and called out, "Come on, just ignore it!"

I couldn't. The dog just stood its ground and barked, snarling, saliva flailing off its fangs.

The owner, after what seemed an eternity, came out to see what had exasperated her pet to the point of hysteria and called it back inside. Only then could I move, dripping perspiration, Barbie laughing! *Laughing?*

The source of my near death experience? A Chihuahua. A Chihuahua with a pink bow in its collar.

Was my life in mortal danger? No. Could I have carried on my way? Yes. Did this situation look totally bizarre to my fiancée and the demonic dog's owner? Totally! Anxiety can be paralysing.

Since this my wife and I have had pets, including dogs. In fact, I prefer dogs to other animals. A year or so after the Chihuahua-gate I was taken through what some have come to call 'deliverance ministry' by a very sweet eighty-year-old woman called Phyllis Greenslade in the church we attended. Among other things she talked through my fear of dogs and prayed into this with me. Since then I have loved dogs. I show bona fide guard dogs a healthy respect; but this seems to be common sense to me, not an irrational fear.

Beyond Anxious

Jesus knew anxiety beyond anything you and I will ever know. He is fully God, fully man. Theologians call this the hypostatic union, where Christ's divinity and humanity are joined in one individual existence or hypostasis. Within the Gospels we see evidence of His divinity; He commands nature to obey, walks on water, heals the incurable, turns water into wine, is worshipped, even raises people from the dead. We also see His humanity. Nothing portrays this more clearly in the Gospels than the events leading up to and including the crucifixion. For Christians it is easier to see Jesus as divine, supernatural. Yet in submitting to God's will Jesus intentionally made Himself vulnerable. He had to experience trials, temptations and ultimately death as a man to bring you victory in the areas where your humanity fails.[175]

When Jesus faced anxiety, I do not mean this in the sense that He worried and therefore sinned. He didn't worry about the daily things in life, like what to wear or what to eat. He instructs you to join Him in this peace, that God will provide for all your needs, just as Jesus' needs were provided for by God.[176] I am talking about an anxiety that is very intense, a personal crisis that takes a person beyond that which is bearable, bringing on an involuntary physiological response. Jesus went beyond what is humanly bearable so that your unbearable burden can be lifted. This is recorded for us in the Gospels:

> *And being in anguish, he prayed more earnestly, and his sweat was like drops of blood falling to the ground.*[177]

There are a few key words and phrases here: "anguish", "more earnestly", "sweat like blood". Jesus experienced incredibly deep anguish whilst in prayer. He has asked God if there was any other way! Fathoming what Jesus was experiencing at that moment is impossible. The depth of the turmoil and the depth of restraint He was showing is incredible. He is fully God after all; He could call down fire from heaven and destroy those who were plotting to kill Him.[178]

Jesus prays *more earnestly.* He keeps going back to the Father. Asking, pleading, and re-submitting Himself each time to the Father's

---

175 Hebrews 2:18, 4:15.

176 Matthew 6:25-34.

177 Luke 22:44.

178 Luke 9:54 – Jesus actually rebuked James and John for suggesting this, showing that it was possible to do this but was not God's way. During this dispensation people have the opportunity to repent.

will. This is the way, the only way, salvation can come. Through the sacrifice of the Innocent One.

Some Friends You Are!

Matthew, in his retelling, gives further insight into the anguish Jesus is feeling:

> *Then he said to them, "My soul is overwhelmed with sorrow to the point of death. Stay here and keep watch with me."*[179]

Jesus describes Himself as being overwhelmed, to the point of death. This is not hyperbole, exaggeration or flippancy. Jesus is clearly describing the growing knowledge that the hour is fast approaching when He will die. He asks His friends to pray for Him and to support Him.

Three times they fall asleep; they are tired, after all!

It is often said that in a crisis you will find out who your friends are. It is not that the disciples are bad people. They have left everything to follow Jesus: businesses, a steady income, family and friends. They have given up much to be with Him. They have done more than most others.[180] Even so, three times they fall asleep when Jesus is praying.[181] His best friends start to let Him down in the hour of His greatest need.

Jesus knows what it feels like when your friends let you down in your darkest hour. It is not that your friends are bad people or selfish; they have busy lives and, being human, a limited capacity to love and to give. Do not burn bridges because they have not come through in the last few strides of the marathon that they have run with you. Be gracious, loving and forgiving. They may not even know that you feel the way you do because, like Jesus, the most earnest prayers that you pray are prayed in a Gethsemane, away from prying eyes. This was the beginning of the scattering of the disciples around the events of the crucifixion. They eventually return and are restored. Your friends will too. Friendship cannot be seen from just the standpoint of the

---

[179] Matthew 26:38.
[180] John 6:60-71.
[181] Matthew 26:36-46.

one demanding it; the best friends are not always those who walk with you through the difficult times and say what you want to hear. True friends will tell you the truth even when you do not want to hear it. The truth is that sometimes there will be things in life that you will face alone, except for the presence of Jesus.[182]

Jesus knows what this is like. He walked there before you.

Blood, Sweat and Tears

Luke, as I mentioned, says Jesus' sweat became blood-like. Luke was not present. He is not one of the disciples. He is a doctor, a careful researcher who is writing to a Roman official named Theophilus.[183] What Luke is describing is hematohidrosis, where sweat appears to be droplets of blood. This is an extremely rare condition. Even though Luke is a doctor, he has probably never witnessed it himself. Most doctors today would not see hematohidrosis. It is probably included by Luke because of his medical background; he knows that it exists.

Researchers today have identified that this is caused by acute fear and intense mental contemplation.[184] Intense mental contemplation is exactly what Jesus has described: "My soul is overwhelmed with sorrow to the point of death." There have been six cases of this condition reported in modern times of those on death row.[185] Jesus is on a death row of a different kind. There is only one person on it. He is about to be betrayed by a friend. He is about to be tortured and killed in the most horrendous and humiliating way known to man. He is about to carry the sins of all humanity. He is about to die for you, for your sins, for your redemption. In His vulnerability, humanity and anguish He sweats blood.

Jesus went through this so that you could endure and survive. Whatever you are facing, Jesus has been there, lived through those emotions, submitted to God's will and has overcome! This does not

---

182 Proverbs 18:24.

183 Luke 1:3; Acts 1:1; Colossians 4:14.

184 MLA H. R. Jerajani et al. *Hematohidrosis – A Rare Clinincal Phenomenon;* Indian Journal of Dermatology; 54.3 (2009): 290–292. PMC. Web. 18/03/15.

185 ibid.

trivialise your own anguish and suffering. It recognises how important it is for Father God; for He wanted to secure freedom through Christ for you. He allows Jesus to suffer, to be vulnerable, to be exposed to the depths of sorrow, so that He can give you beauty for ashes, joy for mourning and praise instead of heaviness.[186] Thank God that in the midst of your trials Jesus brings peace.

[186] Isaiah 61:3.

PART FIVE

He Bleeds

Once you were alienated from God and were enemies in your minds because of your evil behaviour. But now he has reconciled you by Christ's physical body through death to present you holy in his sight, without blemish and free from accusation – if you continue in your faith, established and firm, and do not move from the hope held out in the gospel.

Colossians 1:21-23a

Yet it was the Lord's will to crush him and
cause him to suffer, and though the Lord
makes his life an offering for sin, he will see
his offspring and prolong his days, and the
will of the Lord will prosper in his hand.

Isaiah 53:10

CHAPTER FOURTEEN

The Sacrifice of Jesus

I have heard the sacrifice of Jesus described as many things: a price paid to the devil; a symbolic gesture by God; some have even said anyone could have died for our sins. None of these are correct. There was no deal with the devil at the cross. He did not want Jesus to be the sacrifice for sins. This is why he tempted Him, for if Jesus could have been made to sin, He would not have been the perfect sacrifice required by law. If anything, the devil is a legalist who bends the rules to his own ends. Stopping the crucifixion would have been on his agenda if he had realised that through Jesus' death forgiveness would come to you. The idea that that cross is a symbolic gesture, a purely spiritualised event that need not have taken place, is also wrong. Jesus had to die. There was no other way to restore us to God. Only Jesus could die for your sins. He is the only perfect man to have ever walked the earth. The sacrifice that was required had to be pure and holy.

For Christians, their hearts break when they hear Jesus' name dragged through the mud, used as a swear word and maligned. They know something about Jesus that is only known from the perspective of the cross where they stand with sins forgiven: Jesus was accused, spat on, tortured, humiliated and ultimately crucified in their place. He came to take that for us. He is still being treated with scorn for He is the eternal sacrifice. He does not need defending for He has proven His divinity by being raised from the dead although He is still reproached by humanity.

Jesus fulfilled each and every requirement that God had for the perfect sacrifice. No one else could fulfil this criterion. No one else ever has. The terms of your behaviour can be negotiated with God until the proverbial cows come home, but you will never change the fact that it is God who is offended, that sin separates you from His love and presence, and that restitution has to be made. It was a price we could not pay. It was a price too high for us to consider.

This book would be incomplete without looking at why the cross was needed.

Whichever Way You Look at It, It's Still a Cross

People will often question the Gospel accounts of what happened the day Jesus was crucified. They will say there are too many contradictions, too many variances in the different accounts, for the events of Good Friday to actually be true. What such detractors forget, or chose to ignore, is that the different ways the story of the cross are told actually reinforce its trustworthiness.

When evidence is considered by the police making a case their investigation will look for contradictions and inconsistencies in the testimony of the eye witnesses. They will also be alarmed if everyone's testimony is identical for it sounds contrived and rehearsed. Barbie and I once witnessed a car crash. We were directly behind an American muscle car at a set of traffic lights. The lights turned green and it set off accelerating hard. As it did it was sideswiped by someone who had run through their red light. In the ensuing investigation our statements were taken by the police independently. Our main facts tied up: yes, the light had turned green; yes, the other vehicle definitely hit the car; yes, this person was driving. We disagreed on the minor things: how fast were they going at the time; did anyone sound their horns; did anyone brake prior to impact? These variances proved, rather than disproved, the statements we gave. They were not rehearsed, planned or contrived. They were honest recollections as we saw them. It should be no surprise that there are divergences between the four Gospel accounts.

People think the Bible is all about them. It is not. It is about the brokenness of God's heart and His love that overflows to you. Some think that they were created for God to experience love. That's not true. Within the Godhead there was always love. The Father loves the Son and the Spirit. The Son loves the Father and the Spirit. The Spirit loves the Father and the Son. When they in unison said, "Let us create them in our own image,"[187] it was not from a lack of love or a need to experience love. You were created from an *overflow* of love. The Trinitarian God has so much love that He desires to share it with others outside of Himself. He loves so much, so powerfully, so passionately that this love needed further expression and literally overflowed from the Trinity. This is God's very nature.

The Bible reminds us that, "Whoever does not love does not know God, because God *is* love."[188] It is a four letter definition of who He is. Every illustration for love, every synonym, every possibility and all your experiences of love should point you to the reality of who He is and what you are missing in life. Love. Unquenchable, stubborn, irrepressible love. He loves with an everlasting love. The Psalmist declares:

> *I will sing of the LORD's great love forever; with my mouth I will make your faithfulness known through all generations. I will declare that your love stands firm forever.*[189]

The New Testament's special word for God's love is *agape,* an unconditional love that is undeserved yet freely given. The Old Testament has a special way of describing God's love too. Jeremiah 31:3 describes this love as being an everlasting love; in the Hebrew the word combination implies a mother's unending love for a child. The prophet elaborates by saying this love is expressed through unfailing kindness; which carries the idea in the original text of a resolute stubbornness in the love displayed by Him to His children. It lasts forever in the way a love for a child in a mother's heart only grows, never ceasing. He has made His mind up to love you and not

---

[187] Genesis 1:26.

[188] 1 John 4:8, emphasis mine.

[189] Psalm 89:1-2a.

to turn His face from you. He may not approve of all the actions you take. He calls you to repentance and will even, from time to time, discipline you as any good parent will.[190]

In all things His love for you is the motivation. God's love stays faithful to us long after we've forfeited any claim to His love. God's love is a binding kind of love, a love that refuses to give up.

That means God has not given up on you yet!

God's 'stubborn love' is described by the apostle Paul:

> *Who shall separate us from the love of Christ? Shall trouble or hardship or persecution or famine or nakedness or danger or sword? As it is written: "For your sake we face death all day long; we are considered as sheep to be slaughtered." No, in all these things we are more than conquerors through him who loved us. For I am convinced that neither death nor life, neither angels nor demons, neither the present nor the future, nor any powers, neither height nor depth, nor anything else in all creation, will be able to separate us from the love of God that is in Christ Jesus our Lord.*[191]

God stubbornly refuses to ever stop loving you.

That love was perfectly displayed between God the Father and Adam the first man in the Garden of Eden. Their relationship was perfect. It was uninterrupted. God and Adam would commune together. They would talk for hours uninterrupted. Adam would tell God all about his day, how he had named things, how he had explored the garden, how he and Eve were enjoying their lives.

There was no shame, no sin, no guilt, no barrier between them and the overflowing love of God. They knew His uninterrupted presence. God was everywhere.[192] At special times God would literally manifest Himself, an epiphany as it were, by walking through the garden. They could look upon Him at this time and not fear His glory, for mankind reflected that glory and that love. Adam's prayers were uninhibited and God would hear him talking, praying,

---

190 Hebrews 12:7-11.

191 Romans 8:35-38.

192 Psalm 139.

constantly communicating with his Father. It was beautiful. It was good.

Silence! The joy of the Godhead was interrupted. Adam's voice had been muted. Immediately the Father came looking. Adam and Eve had hidden themselves out of fear and shame after their sin had entered the perfect world. The cry of God, "Where are you?" had nothing to do with geography. God knew where they were hiding.[193] He could see beyond the shrubs, trees and bushes to where they were physically. The question was prompted by the silence. Adam had stopped seeking God and instead had started fleeing Him. He had stopped praying and had remained tight-lipped. He had stopped entering into God's presence and started hiding. God's question was the cry of anguish of a love rejected. He was heartbroken.

God loves perfectly. Justice had to be seen to be in action too. A Father's love without discipline is not love; it is an insipid indulgence of the one who is wrong. True love seeks justice for the continual benefit of the one who is loved. As Adam and Eve now stood before God, dressed in their attempt to cover their shame, which actually proved their shame, the holiness of God first became apparent to them. They had believed a lie that had said they would be like Him if they ate from the tree of knowledge of good and evil. The truth was that they had already been like God – sinless. Now they suddenly understood what holiness was, for they had lost theirs and were confronted by the Holy God. They had fallen. The presence of God, once taken for granted, once enjoyed and anticipated, was now actually detrimental to their health! They would die! Their bodies already had the very beginnings of decay, although in God's graciousness for them, it would take hundreds of years for physical death to come. They were tarnished.

God's love had to be expressed. His love was still inextinguishable but had been rejected. The Father looked to the Son. The Son nodded in agreement. He knew the Father was going to give humanity to Him. He would walk with them as Father had. The Son would have to be hidden from the Father, as Adam and Eve were hidden too, so that humanity could enter back into the presence of God, never to be cut off again. A way had to be made. The Spirit hovered and instantly

---

193 Genesis 3:9.

knew, in the way they each instantly knew the mind and heart of the other, that one day He would reside within the hearts of men and women. Justice would be fulfilled.

He could wipe out the fledgling human race, start again. Who would know? Except the Godhead. *They* would know. They knew that the free will they had created within Adam and Eve, that had chosen to reject Father's love, needed to remain intact. They had not sought to create automatons, but those who would freely choose to love the Father as the Godhead freely chose to love each other. Love had been rejected but had to be accepted freely too. Love knowingly accepted would be a reciprocal love.

Adam and Eve began to blame each other and then the serpent, the manifestation of the devil. God glanced over to the serpent, there proudly on its four legs smirking back at the Creator. A new brazenness in its demeanour; it now had the keys of sin and death.

A New World Order

The order of things had changed. Before, when God would come to Eden, He would converse with Adam. That was the order of authority in Eden. God had given dominion to him.[194] What was good had now been corrupted.

God first speaks to the deceiver:

> *So the Lord God said to the snake, "Because you have done this, 'Cursed are you above all livestock and all wild animals! You will crawl on your belly and you will eat dust all the days of your life. And I will put enmity between you and the woman, and between your offspring and hers; he will crush your head, and you will strike his heel.'"* [195]

---

[194] Genesis 1:26. We may read this and struggle with the idea of the patriarchal nature of the Jewish writings and Christianity as a whole. Whilst there is clearly room for equality in the Church and a Kingdom mentality (Galatians 3:28), we also have to accept that God has revealed Himself as Father and this love is demonstrated through the patriarchal nature of our faith.

[195] Genesis 3:14-15.

In these verses is an unusual curse, that the snake would slither. Whilst many people will find these creatures to be enigmatically beautiful, others will find them repulsive because of their association with the Genesis account. This does not mean that snakes are literally the devil. The devil appears as a snake in the Garden. They became a reminder to humanity that there is a devil. This also raises the question, did snakes ever have legs?

Archaeologists since have discovered a four-legged snake, the rather fetchingly named *Tetrapodophis amplectus.*[196] For years scientists have questioned the evidence of the Bible but this discovery undergirds the biblical account; there were once snakes that potentially walked, now there are not. The biblical evidence would indicate that there were indeed walking snakes that went 'backwards' evolutionarily speaking because they were to be a reminder in the psyche of humankind of what was lost at the Fall.

Genesis 3:15 contains the first promise that God was going to intervene, to make a way for mankind to return to Him, and that this way would come through a man: Jesus! God would not leave humanity destitute with no hope. There would be a reconciliation. Reading through this account carefully, there is no hint of any deal being struck with the devil. The price to be paid was to rightfully see God's justice prevail. It was God's wrath at the rejection of His love and presence that had to be made right. That would not happen by bowing to the devil in any way, even though the enemy now had the dominion that was Adam's and now had the keys of sin and death. Someone was going to have to claim those keys as their own. A man, a perfect man, a righteous man, a second Adam, would come and take those keys right out of the hands of the devil. That man would be called Immanuel, 'God with us'![197]

God then turns to the woman at that moment, for it was her succumbing to deception that led Adam to sin. He says:

---

[196] http://www.the-scientist.com/?articles.view/articleNo/43604/title/Four-legged-SnakeFossil-Found/, accessed 04/08/15.
Scientists believe this proves a link between snakes and lizards. Evidence is always open to interpretation through the lens of the interpreter.

[197] Isaiah 7:14.

"I will make your pains in childbearing very severe; with painful labour you will give birth to children. Your desire will be for your husband, and he will rule over you." [198]

Is this the unkindest of punishments? What would have been easy for a woman has now become difficult. Childbirth is one of the most beautiful things a woman can experience; for some it is also one of the most dreaded. It hurts. My wife's a nurse and, after more than twenty years in this role, retrained as a midwife. She loves it. She could tell stories about childbirth that no woman would want to hear! There are those who claim a woman can go pain-free with hypnosis or Eastern meditation. There's also New Age propaganda about being pain-free during childbirth. The fact is some women will cope better and some will not. It is more down to the fact of how a woman prepares her body for labour – the very word implies hard work – than anything else.

It was after this that Adam actually named his wife Eve, for she would be the giver of life. Eve means 'living' or 'life-giver'.[199]

This verse announces the beginning of the strife between man and woman, perhaps the seeds of hyper-feminism. Please do not throw this book away just yet! When women petition for the same salaries as men in the same jobs they are right to do so. When they campaigned for the vote in the suffragette movement they were right to do so. There is equality in the Kingdom. What is equality? Equality is not being the same. Men and women are physiologically and biologically different. They are not the same. There is equality before God. He loves all His children the same but equality is not the same as function. In Genesis it is clear that the woman would despise the rule of her man. Man would misuse that rule. What was perfect before the Fall, what was good, would now be corrupted and would become despised. God addressed her before the man. There would always be struggle between them outside of God's love.

Finally, to Adam He said:

"Because you listened to your wife and ate fruit from the tree about which I commanded you, 'You must not eat

---

198 Genesis 3:16.
199 Genesis 3:20.

> *from it,' 'Cursed is the ground because of you; through painful toil you will eat food from it all the days of your life. It will produce thorns and thistles for you, and you will eat the plants of the field. By the sweat of your brow you will eat your food until you return to the ground, since from it you were taken; for dust you are and to dust you will return.'"*[200]

If you are reading this as a woman you might think that Adam got off lightly, but it strikes at the very core of being what a man is: a provider. This may seem archaic and outdated to some because society has lost the image of godly manhood. What is at the heart of a male psyche is more than just machoism and a love for sports. Men were created to show a typology of the provision of God our Great Provider. That is why even today when a man is unable to provide for his family due to unemployment, disability or any manner of other reasons, he will struggle with his very identity. His worth has been stripped away in his eyes. This is nothing to do with the amount that is earned, but that earning is happening.

It is not that these things would not affect a woman; they affect her differently. Women tend to have a 'get-on-with-it-at-all-costs' attitude. Unfairly called the weaker sex, women have an incredible strength within them.

If a man cannot provide he will crumble. He will need love and support. Ultimately he will need a job! He needs to be doing. We see this in church life all the time. Few men will come to a prayer meeting, but run a building project or refurbishment at church and there is no shortage of men, even non-Christian men, who want to get involved. Twice in my life I have experienced the pain of redundancy, and on both occasions there was a crisis of purpose.

Man was given work to do before the Fall. He had dominion and had to tend the Garden. After the Fall what was easy became difficult. It became a chore, a duty and hard work. It was rewarded differently. Weeds and thistles would grow where once crops would grow. The very task would war against Adam. He would need to become a conqueror and resolute. He was going to have to work hard

[200] Genesis 3:17-19.

all of his days. Every day would be a day to conquer. Paradise was over.

A Sign of Things to Come

> *The Lord God made garments of skin for Adam and his wife and clothed them. And the Lord God said, "The man has now become like one of us, knowing good and evil. He must not be allowed to reach out his hand and take also from the tree of life and eat, and live for ever." So the Lord God banished him from the Garden of Eden to work the ground from which he had been taken. After he drove the man out, he placed on the east side of the Garden of Eden cherubim and a flaming sword flashing back and forth to guard the way to the tree of life.*[201]

These punitive measures, that would affect the whole of the world and everyone born thereafter, broke God's heart.

Whilst God's anger needs to be appeased, He tempers this with love. He makes Adam and Eve garments. He still provides. They had tried to cover their own shame with their attempt at fashion design. Leaves covered them.[202] Today nothing has changed. Many will deny their shame. They will 'cover' it with celebration and the notion that all should enjoy what they have become. All these things are just modern day fig leaves. God, though, did something different. He made them coverings of animal skins. Not only were these more practical for life outside of the protection of Eden, they began to tell the story that without the shedding of blood there can be no forgiveness of sins.[203]

Shame is a feeling. It was clearly felt in Eden as Adam and Eve tried to hide from God, covering themselves. Shame may not be felt by everyone today as they take pride within themselves. Guilt is a fact. It does not depend upon feelings. God knew this. He covers their guilt with animal skins because there is life in the blood. The whole process of obtaining forgiveness must be done on God's terms.

---

[201] Genesis 3:21-24.
[202] Genesis 3:7.
[203] Hebrews 9:22.

In the Old Testament a foreshadow of the greatest sacrifice known would be instigated with the sacrificial system of the Jewish nation, under God's direction, so that sins could be put aside, even temporarily, to give hope to people. Ultimately this system would be insufficient because it could never deal with the root problem, that a man had fallen and, therefore, a man would need to come and live a perfect life before God. The most precious of all sacrifices was that of the pure lamb. Jesus was the Lamb promised in the Old Testament.

God then banishes them from the Garden. He does this not as a further punishment but for their protection and the protection of the whole of Creation. If they remained and then ate of another tree, the tree of life, they would live forever in their sin. There was another tree planned in the heart of God, a tree where the Life-giver Himself would hang and die, to enable eternal life, life beyond this one. An eternity of sins forgiven and innocence restored. Innocence is to do with 'not being guilty' but is also the purity of never having committed a wrong. This is what the Bible calls *justification;* you will stand before God as just, righteous, pure, holy and whole. An eternity with Father, Son and Spirit in perfect, undiluted fellowship and communion with all those who accept Jesus as their Lord and Saviour. Taking of the tree of life in the Garden would have led to a perverted and selfish immortality, one that was based upon sin and lawlessness and not grace and love. Adam and Eve were not prohibited from eternal life before this, for there were two special trees in Eden: the tree of knowledge of good and evil and the tree of life. It was only from the former that they were forbidden to eat.[204]

Eternal life was always in God's agenda. It still is. That life, though, had to be lived in holiness and in communion with God. Outside of that it becomes life, but not a life that is full and abundant. It's merely eternal existence. Once they had committed sin, eternal life would need to be offered again but only through One who was sinless. Banishing them from the Garden, protecting the supernatural life that could be gained there, was to leave a door open for you to accept eternal life again by looking to another tree displayed for all in a place of death, Golgotha.

---

[204] Genesis 2:16.

CHAPTER FIFTEEN

Caiaphas' Story

Caiaphas was the High Priest at the time of Jesus' trial. He is mentioned nine times by name in the Gospels and Acts and was a powerful figure of the day in Judea.[205] In fact, next to Pilate, he held the most influence in the region. Appointed by Rome to help control the Jews he served for a period of eighteen years, demonstrating his political savvy as well as his dominance of the religious community.[206]

He's no fool. After the resurrection of Lazarus he can see that this insurgent Jesus is going to overthrow the religious-political balance and that something must be done. Caiaphas, at a specifically convened council of the Sanhedrin, puts forward the idea that Jesus must die.

The Sanhedrin were the religious court made up of up to seventy-one male city leaders including, it seems, the High Priest, who could accuse lawbreakers but without two witnesses could not initiate arrests.[207]

Even then, although he is vehemently opposed to Jesus and wants Him dead to protect himself, as High Priest he prophesies that Jesus

---

[205] Matthew 26:3,57; Luke 3:2; John 11:49, 18:13,14,24,28; Acts 4:6.

[206] Jackson, W, Caiaphas – *Official at the Trial of Jesus,* article online, https://www.christiancourier.com/articles/664-caiaphas-official-at-the-trial-of-jesus, accessed 19/08/15.

[207] Schoenberg, S, *The Sanhedrin,* article online, https://www.jewishvirtuallibrary.org/jsource/Judaism/Sanhedrin.html, accessed 19/08/15.

will die for the Jews and the Gentiles.[208] God can even use enemies to speak truth!

Illegitimate Authority

Throughout the New Testament Caiaphas is referred to as the High Priest. It is not clear if all the Jews actually recognised him as such. In John 18:13 and Acts 4:6 another High Priest is mentioned, Annas, who was actually the father-in-law of Caiaphas. Some would say this is a clear contradiction in the Bible and therefore we should discount the whole of it. Luke actually goes as far as to combine the two and says that John was baptising during the high priesthood of Annas and Caiaphas.[209]

There can only be one High Priest at a time and this role is for life. So why isn't Annas serving as High Priest? Annas served as High Priest from A.D. 7-15 at which point he was forcibly removed by the then Roman procurator Valerius Gratus and replaced with Caiaphas. It is probable that many of the Jews regarded Annas to be the legitimate office holder, hence the references to him as High Priest.[210] Everyone knew that Caiaphas was an illegitimate High Priest, for the priesthood was chosen from the Levitical line and the High Priest was a non-political post.

Until Caiaphas, it seems. At this point in Jewish history the priesthood had seemingly broken down to some degree, acquiescing to the demands of their oppressors, probably for their own survival.

The Kangaroo Court

When brought before Caiaphas, this renegade authority figure, everyone in the room would have known what the intended outcome was. In the face of this is the most incredible statement by Jesus: *silence!*

> *Those who had arrested Jesus took him to Caiaphas, the high priest, where the teachers of the law and the elders*

---

[208] John 11:45-53, especially verses 51-53.

[209] Luke 3:2.

[210] Jackson, W, Caiaphas – *Official at the Trial of Jesus,* article online, https://www.christiancourier.com/articles/664-caiaphas-official-at-the-trial-of-jesus, accessed 19/08/15.

> *had assembled; Peter followed him at a distance, right up to the courtyard of the high priest. He entered and sat down with the guards to see the outcome. The chief priests and the whole Sanhedrin were looking for false evidence against Jesus so that they could put him to death. They did not find any, even though many false witnesses came forward. Finally two came forward and declared Jesus had claimed He would destroy and rebuild the Temple in three days. Infuriated Caiaphas demanded an answer but Jesus remained silent.*[211]

This is a glimpse of the Sanhedrin at work as a religious court. They are desperately trying to find two corroborating witnesses that will be the undoing of Jesus. They cannot find any until two come forward with something of the semblance of truth, but their testimony is not enough to convict Jesus of a crime that requires a death penalty, for it is not wholly true. Jesus had been talking about His own body, how He would die and be raised to life in three days, not the physical building. Even though these two agreed it is likely that the witnesses were paid stooges, practised and rehearsed, who were after a quick pay day.

When questioned over these allegations Jesus remains silent. He is going to die. He is not going to die for a lie. He is going to sacrifice Himself for God's purpose of redeeming these very accusers who are trying to entrap Him.

Finally, Caiaphas can take this silence no longer. Does Jesus not know who he is? He is the High Priest! Surely even this Jesus has to respect that. What Caiaphas does not know is that standing before him is the true High Priest. The one who has immoral authority accuses the One moral authority. The one who holds supposititious power challenges the One with authentic power. The one who has unlawfully obtained position goads the One who fulfilled the law. The one who has grasped for prestige attacks the One who laid down His place to die for sinners.[212]

Caiaphas finally invokes the court oath, the oath before the living God; the oath under which all evidence before them is supposed to be

---

[211] Matthew 26:57-58.
[212] Philippians 2:6-11.

uttered, and before the God whose name they have taken in vain by hearing all the spurious evidence previously before them, demanding that Jesus will tell them the truth!

> *The high priest said to him, "I charge you under oath by the living God: Tell us if you are the Christ, the Son of God." "Yes, it is as you say," Jesus replied. "But I say to all of you: In the future you will see the Son of Man sitting at the right hand of the Mighty One and coming on the clouds of heaven." Then the high priest tore his clothes and said, "He has spoken blasphemy! Why do we need any more witnesses? Look, now you have heard the blasphemy. What do you think?"*[213]

Jesus, if He remained silent at this juncture, would have probably been released. It is not a death wish that brings this confession from Jesus – the events in Gethsemane prove this – but rather it is a declaration, identification and prophecy.

Declared Messiah – Would the Real High Priest Step Forward?

The declaration had to be made before the High Priest that the Messiah had come. This is vitally important, for Caiaphas had been dicing with death himself for years. A High Priest could die within the Holy of Holies if there was sin present. It has long been said that they would wear a rope around the waist or ankle, so that if they died in God's presence they could be dragged out. However, there is no recorded evidence for this and it is likely a legend.[214] The death penalty for sin before God was enshrined in the Old Testament Mosaic Law. Hebrews 9:7 states that the High Priest entered the Holy of Holies under the covering of a blood sacrifice, for his sins and for the sins of the nation, annually.[215] Even Caiaphas would have

---

213 Matthew 26:63b-66.

214 *Did The High Priest Enter the Holy of Holies with a Rope Around His Ankle?* http://www.christiananswers.net/q-eden/anklerope.html, accessed 19/08/15. It may have been a practice in the middle ages in a synagogue.

215 Hebrews 9:7: "But only the high priest entered the inner room, and that only once a year, and never without blood, which he offered for himself and for the sins the people had committed in ignorance." See also Hebrews 10:3-4.

gone through the ritual. In the fifteen or so times he had done this he had come out alive; he had performed a ceremony perfectly adequately, meeting the requisite dress code and sacrifices.[216] His survival was due to the grace of God rather than his ability to meet the Mosaic Law's requirements. God was gracious even to Caiaphas. I doubt, though, he ever encountered the presence of the living God in that sacred place for God was standing before him, and had been walking the earth for the last thirty-three years.

Now He declares to Caiaphas' face that he is standing before the very One whom he prophesied about when the plot to trap Jesus began.

The subtext here would not have been lost on the scheming High Priest: you have stood before God giving sacrifices for your sins without repentance and now the perfect sacrifice stands before you for your sins!

In the declaration Caiaphas instantly knows that Jesus is claiming to be the true High Priest.

Messiah Identified – I Am

There is also identification, for Jesus has to make it plain to everyone hearing: He is God. The simple words, "Yes, it is as you say," show Caiaphas, by answering the question as a statement, that he himself has confessed that Jesus is God.

Jesus could have just said, "No, not me. Mistaken identity." He did not. He stands before a kangaroo court and places Himself in the hands of men who want Him dead.

King David, when given a choice, chose not to be placed into the hands of men bent on revenge but rather chose to be in the hands of God.[217] Jesus here is making the choice of obedience to God's plan and will. The One who created the hands of men takes Himself out of the hands of God, a place He has been for all His earthly life, and puts Himself into the hands of the created.

---

216 Exodus 28.

217 2 Samuel 24:13-14.

Messiah Prophesies – If You're Going to Prophesy, Finish It!

Jesus prophesies too. It is this that Caiaphas reacts to so strongly. There is no ambiguity here either:

> *"But I say to all of you: In the future you will see the Son of Man sitting at the right hand of the Mighty One and coming on the clouds of heaven."*

Jesus prophesies His resurrection and His return. In no uncertain terms He tells them all that He is God. What's more, He completes the prophecy that Caiaphas gave before the very court in which He now stands accused. Put these two scriptures together and this is how it reads:

> *"You know nothing at all! You do not realise that it is better for you that one man die for the people than that the whole nation perish."*[218]

> *"But I say to all of you: In the future you will see the Son of Man sitting at the right hand of the Mighty One and coming on the clouds of heaven."*[219]

When Caiaphas prophesied it was incomplete. The whole truth had to be laid before the Sanhedrin. Jesus would die at their hands, but God would raise Him up. Caiaphas' bones have since been discovered by archaeologists, but Jesus' would never be discovered for He would rise from the dead![220]

The King of Glory Made Vulnerable

The high priest is obsessed and filled with rage. His ability to sway his peers is fully on show now, his political prowess at full force. His fury at being outwitted by Jesus unabated, he moves for a judgement:

> *Then the high priest tore his clothes and said, "He has spoken blasphemy! Why do we need any more witnesses? Look, now you have heard the blasphemy. What do you*

---

218 John 11:49-50.
219 Matthew 26:64.
220 See note (iv) in 'Additional Notes' on page 241.

> *think?" "He is worthy of death," they answered. Then they spit in his face and struck him with their fists. Others slapped him and said, "Prophesy to us, Christ. Who hit you?"* [221]

Judgement is pronounced. No more witnesses. He deserves death. They begin to ridicule Him, spit on Him and slap Him. These three things are the ultimate contempt that they can show. To mock someone is not pleasant. It is a verbal attack. Their anger continues to grow as they spit upon Jesus. Not just one or two would spit; as part of their judgement, all, over seventy of them, would take in turns spitting on the perfect One. Spitting was seen as something unclean. Even today it is not regarded as pleasant. For them to spit in Jesus' face showed the out-and-out contempt they had for Him. They then slapped Him, although the Greek word used is *kolaphizo,* meaning with knuckles or a closed fist.[222] Again they probably all had the opportunity to show their anger at Jesus in this way; in fact, to have not reacted in front of their peers may have been interpreted as at best mercy, at worst agreement with the accused.

Their fervour reaches a fever pitch as they goad Jesus to identify who struck Him, an indication that by this time He is blindfolded.[223] Jesus is rejected and beaten, humiliated by those He came to save. He does not change direction or tack when under this scrutiny. Worse is still to come.

When vilified by those who should know better you will often break under the demoralisation. *People should know better.* They do but they still do wrong. All you have control of in this kind of circumstance is your own attitude, your own character response, your own equilibrium. People cannot steal your peace. Nor can the devil. Peace, among many others things, was secured for you on the cross. You can give it away though, hand it over to accusers and naysayers. Jesus did not. His security was in who He was and also in His destiny in God. Remember everything He gave for you. Emulate His attitude, His demeanour, His purposeful intention in a crisis. Paul reminds the

---

221 Matthew 26:65-68.

222 R.H. Mounce, *Matthew,* NIBC, Massachusetts: Hendrickson (1991); 248.

223 Mark 14:65.

Philippian church that their attitude should be the same as that of Jesus;[224] so should yours. It's hard. It's not for the fainthearted, the weak-willed and those concerned with their own comfort. The rewards outstrip the torment of the current moment. Be strong, be lamb-like, be Christ-like. Jesus placed Himself in the hands of men so that you would never have to be out of the hand of God.

224 Philippians 2:5-11.

CHAPTER SIXTEEN

Pilate's Story

Everyone has heard of Pontius Pilate. His story is found in Matthew 27:11-26 and Luke 23:1-15,18-25.

Pilate was nearing the end of his life; he would die a few years after the events surrounding the crucifixion, although he did not know it at this time. He was a Roman equestrian, equivalent to a knight, of the Samnite clan of Pontii, hence the title Pontius. His appointment as prefect of Judea was through the intervention of Sejanus, a favourite of the then emperor Tiberius. It is unlikely that he would have been appointed without the protection and sponsorship of his political ally.

During his governorship he attracted the enmity of the Jewish populace, holding their religion in disdain by hanging images of the Emperor throughout the region and having coins minted depicting profane pagan images. After Sejanus' own demise a few years before the death of Christ, Pilate found himself more exposed politically and at greater odds with the Jews. Holding on to his power became an almost daily struggle. Decisions became more irrational as his insecurities came to the fore. If he could not win people over with fine words or political bribery, he would crush them with cruelty. Caiaphas and the Sanhedrin may well have used this political instability to their advantage when petitioning him to crucify Jesus.[225]

---

[225] John 19:12.

The written record of him in the New Testament and the writings of the historian Josephus are consistent. Pilate seems to be a pragmatist but unsure of how far he can go; doubtful of the level of his authority, yet headstrong, verging on megalomania. He incited both Jews and Samaritans to riot. There was doubt if he could quash rebellions. Josephus observed that in order to abolish Jewish laws, and with the intent of diminishing privileges Jews had hitherto enjoyed, Pilate ordered his troops to encamp in Jerusalem and sent them into the city with images of the Emperor attached to their ensigns. When the Jews demonstrated in Caesarea, Pilate's city of residence, he threatened them with death unless they desisted; but when the Jews showed their readiness to die, he ordered the images removed. Pilate was astounded by their firm resolution and this deeply affected his relationship with the Jews and exposed his own weaknesses.[226]

When Jesus is brought before Pilate he is a ruler struggling to hold on to his power; without the protection of his sponsor, under the watchful eye of Rome, with questions about his ability to deal with the renegade Jewish people who already enjoyed far too many concessions. The scene is set.

Would Pilate agree to crucify Jesus or would he face another rebellion from the Jews? He could not risk an unlawful execution. He certainly would not hold on to power if there were another Jewish uprising. He is a man with few options and no friends.

Are You the King of the Jews?

Perhaps this question from Pilate makes more sense in light of his political history. If Jesus is not a king then this makes the situation containable; if He is a ruler of some description, Pilate must tread carefully.

Jesus has remained mostly silent before the Sanhedrin. Here He gives Pilate the answer he does not want to hear: "Yes, it is as you say!"[227]

This must have chilled Pilate to the very bone. This was no petty criminal, but someone who could bring down his own career.

---

[226] http://www.britannica.com/biography/Pontius-Pilate, accessed 30/12/15.
[227] Matthew 27:11.

Pilate needs a way out. Jesus is not answering further questions. Pilate cannot understand this. He is used to people pleading for leniency. He is accustomed to people bartering, trading their lives for the lives of worse criminals. Jesus is different. He is giving Pilate no way to release Him. He is being… being like a lamb. Yet through this Pilate sees something that has not come to his palace before. He may recognise it from the years on the battlefields where there would have been collateral damage. He may have seen it in his children. He certainly has not seen it before him, silent and unresponsive: *innocence.*

The purity of this Jewish King shrieked in contrast to the crimes Pilate himself had committed in the name of Rome or to protect himself. The blood on his own hands began to cry out before the Lamb of God.

It is the same for everyone. You may not have committed heinous crimes but you have fallen short of God's glory;[228] Jesus' purity overwhelms you when you meet Him as the not-yet-saved. You know this from your own experience and the experience of your loved ones. As you came close to accepting Jesus you were confronted with your own guilt and shame. There are those moments, or some days or even longer, when the struggle with the stark comparison with the sinless Jesus comes to the forefront. You looked for alternatives, just as Pilate did, a way out. Many will try to suppress Jesus' call on their lives. They will reject church as full of hypocrites. They will say the local church only wants their money, their time, another person to brainwash. The truth is, whilst there are many shortcomings in local churches around the world, which saddens me, rejecting Jesus is always going to be at the heart of the issue. It's just convenient to blame it on someone else.

New Ally

Pilate's way out was to send Jesus to Herod. Herod was in Jerusalem at the time and was despised by Pilate. The two did not get on. This Herod is not the Herod of the nativity, but Herod Antipas, his successor. He is the one who had John the Baptist beheaded. He is a local ruler, his title *tetrarch* meaning 'ruler of a quarter'. Appointed

[228] Romans 3:23.

by Rome, hated by the governor, Herod has little power and little authority. Being ruler of Galilee though, this matter of Jesus falls under his bureaucratic rule. Pilate knows that Herod is a callous and debauched character. Sending him Jesus for a judgement would leave Pilate free of this mess.

According to Luke's Gospel, Herod is thrilled.[229] He has wanted to see this miracle-worker for ages. John the Baptist had been an annoyance, a plaything really, an agitator and opposer of his marriage. Jesus was someone far more entertaining. Maybe He'd perform some parlour tricks. Perhaps it was really John the Baptist raised to life again. He had heard rumours and needed to see for himself.[230] Now Pilate was sending him Jesus. An olive branch. An opportunity to show his loyalty to Pilate and secure a favour for the future perhaps. It was going to be a very good day indeed.

When John was incarcerated, Jesus went straight to Galilee to preach, for this is where John had been imprisoned.[231] Jesus wanted to give hope to the people, but also to John; the Messiah was indeed here. Jesus had deeply grieved the death of His cousin, withdrawing to a solitary place.[232] He had needed to be alone, to have time to grieve the loss of his earthly cousin. It was an acceleration of the times and flung Jesus into the limelight even more. He was now centre stage. Matthew says that people sought Him out. News of His whereabouts travelled fast. In the midst of His grief compassion flowed and the feeding of the five thousand followers took place.

Now Jesus stands before His cousin's murderer: an adulterous killer who wants a performance from Him. One word from Jesus to this regional despot could end Herod's life right there. He could command all the powers of heaven against him. The Jewish rulers are there too. They begin to hurl insults and accusations at Jesus again. They are fearful Herod will be disappointed with Him and simply release Him because He is silent. Instead of condemning Herod, Jesus refuses to answer.

---

229 Luke 23:8.
230 Mark 6:14.
231 Mark 1:14.
232 Matthew 14:12-14.

In situations where you have the opportunity to right a hurt or a wrong from the past, it is tempting to let someone have your opinion served up hot with a helping of bitterness on the side followed by a dessert of a piece of your mind. A sin against you that is suppressed will poison the soul. It will eat away and fester. That rehearsed speech that has been practised over and over; the comments made on social media to get people on your side; the emails sent in haste to someone to defend you. All to make sure someone knows how wrong they were, how they should know better, how they should be put in their place.

Jesus is silent. Not out of disrespect. Nor from a repressed anger. He is silent for two reasons.

Firstly, he has already forgiven Herod. He is trusting in God's plan. He knows one day Herod will stand and have to give an account. He knows that vengeance belongs to Father God.[233] He knows that one day Herod will stand before Him for the Father has entrusted judgement to the Son.[234] All Herod needs to do is confess his sins and accept Jesus and he will be in the Kingdom. Did he ever do so? Doubtful… One day you and I will know for sure in heaven.

The second reason Jesus is silent is to do with a tree. A tree had been prepared in Eden that was forbidden. Adam and Eve's sin began this whole story. Omniscient Father had planted another tree and planned another moment when a tree would be the centre of heaven's attention. This seed had grown true and strong. It had been felled and worked by Roman carpenters into a heavy cross beam. It was to hold the most precious of all of heaven and to have the honour, if it can be called that, of being remembered throughout eternity as a beacon and signpost to the forgiveness of Father. If Jesus had listed the crimes of Herod, Herod would have resorted to his default execution method: beheading. It had to be the tree in God's will. Whatever fads may come and go in the Church, it's still about the old rugged cross. It's about a tree. Jesus is silent for He has an appointment with a tree to reclaim more than image. He has to reclaim humanity from sin and

[233] Deuteronomy 32:35.
[234] John 5:22.

death. He has to be the way for salvation. No shortcuts. *Thy will be done, Father.*[235]

Herod tires of this silence. He misreads it, so mocks Jesus. He has him dressed in a fine robe, mocking Him as a king. Perhaps Pilate sent a message that he was sending him a religious king. Herod does not condemn Jesus – this is how Pilate interprets it – in sending Him back to Pilate.[236]

This newfound cooperation sees a friendship between the two.[237] A new allegiance is formed. New allies. In the tumultuous world of Roman politics the enemy of my enemy is my friend.

There's a Pecking Order

John's Gospel records the details of the events around Pilate and Jesus' meeting a little differently than Matthew, Mark and Luke.[238] This is nothing to worry about, as we have discussed previously about the collation of evidence. The first three Gospels are known as the Synoptic Gospels by commentators. This simply means they contain many of the same stories in a similar order. John's Gospel reads differently. For many this is why it is their favourite Gospel. He includes material the others leave out, not because they were not there or because they thought it less important, but because John saw things differently to them.

He is often physically closer to the action than they were. Take the crucifixion, for example; John is at the foot of the cross. He still fled like the others, but returned first – yes, you guessed it! – recorded in his own retelling![239] There is no reason to doubt him though, for he is entrusted to look after Mary by Jesus. He has a closer friendship with Jesus and often referred to himself in the third person as the "disciple whom Jesus loved".

Some try to twist this through eisogesis and claim Jesus was gay – or, if not Jesus, then John certainly was. The truth is, he referred to himself this way to keep the focus on Jesus and not on himself. It's an

---

235 Matthew 6:10, 26:42.
236 Luke 23:15.
237 Luke 23:12.
238 John 18:33-39.
239 John 19:26.

unusual moniker, but not an unusual literary device in the first century A.D. Peter refers to himself in the third person throughout the Gospel titled Mark; but we know that Mark acted as his scribe to record his story. Paul, the apostle, speaks in the third person of someone taken into heaven and seeing mysteries unspeakable.[240] Most commentators believe that Paul is speaking of himself as the timeframe would marry up with when Paul was stoned and left for dead, yet lived.[241] He almost uses the term commonly used today, "I have a friend," when trying to cover up personal identity. So John uses a strange way to deflect the reader to Jesus and not draw attention to himself. It is doubtful he called himself this publicly, but simply in his Gospel. The furore amongst the disciples would have been more than amusing to read about had John gone about saying, "I'm Jesus' favourite!" They already had argued about who was the greatest disciple; it's human nature in a small team to wonder who is top dog at times, even if it's not voiced. Apparently the disciples had no such misgivings![242] John writes from the perspective of being Jesus' favourite.

Jesus has a magnetism about Him. I would wager, though I am not a gambling man, that there have been times when you have felt like Jesus' favourite, like you are the one whom Jesus loves. Jesus oozes this love and attraction to others.

It is rare to meet someone who has this ability to make you feel like you are the only person in the room. When I lived in South Africa I was employed by a firm that dealt in bottled and compressed gases. They had various sites in the country including extraction, cryogenics and bottling plants. As I was in lower management, I was required to go on a management course and the final session was to be with the CEO. He was made of the stuff of legends in the company. He had left the UK on a four-week exploratory trip to see if there was a market for the parent company's products. He never returned. He stayed and developed one of the most successful companies in the country at that time. When he entered the room everyone paid attention. There were only seven of us there but I was impressed he

---

240 1 Corinthians 12:2-5.

241 Acts 14:19; 2 Corinthians 11:25.

242 Mark 9:34.

had learnt our names and greeted us personally. He sat on the edge of a desk and spent ten minutes outlining the vision for his company, no doubt a monologue polished through delivering it many, many times. When he left he shook us all by the hands, posed for pictures for the company magazine and was gone. I doubt he was a Christian; nothing he said or did alerted my "I'm in the presence of a fellow believer" radar. I knew two things though. One, he had a raw magnetism and it had served him well. Two, I could not wait to get back to work the next day and motivate my guys to up production. Why? I felt like I was the only person in the room. As the saying goes, "People will always forget what you say but will remember how you made them feel."[243] If an earthly CEO could do that for a few minutes, how much more did Jesus do that every single moment of His life – and still does!

This magnetic Jesus stands before Pilate; the secure and the insecure converse. Unlike many around him, Jesus actually recognises Pilate's authority. In a strange way this may be comforting for Pilate. Perhaps he is drawn to Jesus' authority and impressed by His demeanour. Standing before him is a king, no doubt in his mind about that, but one who is already battered and bruised, though gracious and insightful.

Decide for Yourself[244]

Everyone, old or young, good or bad, has to decide for themself about Jesus, and not live on the shirttails of someone else's spirituality. It will not suffice; it is a weakened form of Christianity that permeates local church culture today. How many times have you heard, "I do not need to go to church to be a Christian"? Going to church does not make you a Christian, that's true. It is something that happens as a result of being a Christian.

Being a Christian is more than a spiritual gym membership. Gyms today rely on the people who do not go, rather than those who do go. I was once on a tour of a gym where they wanted to introduce new members to the management and talk about the improvements they

243 This quote has been attributed to numerous people, see www.quoteinvestigator.com/2014/04/06/theyfeel/
244 John 18:33-39.

were going to make. I asked how many came to the gym on a weekly basis; what was the actual footfall? It was a large gym and I expected a good number. The manager said they had an average footfall of one thousand people a week. That is not a thousand individuals, for some may go every day, some just once a week. It is literally how many times their turnstile at the entrance indicates an admission. I then asked how many actual members there were, for a gym of that size could not deliver on their promises with just a footfall of a thousand people a week. Sheepishly grinning, the manager said that they had over six thousand members. Gyms' business plans often rely on people not turning up! They need the cash but do not want the gym to be crowded all of the time. You can be a member of a gym and not go; not so with the church. Every day you have to choose to follow Jesus. It cannot be based on hearsay.

Sometimes people get tired of it all, feeling put upon, valued for what they do rather than who they are. There are many nice people like this. One day they will stand before God where 'being nice' will not cut it.

Trying to be nice does not help Pilate before Jesus as he attempts to placate the situation: "Are you the king of the Jews?"

"Is that your own idea," Jesus asks, "or did others talk to you about me?"[245]

You may hear a lot about Jesus in your lifetime. You will hear His name spoken as a swearword. You will hear His name mentioned in connection with those the media want to portray as radicals and mavericks. You will hear sermons about Him. You may even sing His name in church. Do you just hear these things or do you *know* Him? You cannot live on a second hand revelation of who He is. He is totally God, totally man. Invincible. Paradoxically vulnerable. He is exquisite. You have to know Him for yourself. There is nothing more important in the world today. Nothing! There are lots of important, urgent or good things in our lives: relationships, work, children, marriage, study, education, and careers. All of these and other things are good quests and exciting priorities. When all of those people in your life are gone, when your career ends, your life fades into the ether and your mark on history is considered, there will only be one

---

[245] John 18:33b-34.

thing that truly matters: what did you do with Jesus? The answer to this question will determine your salvation, true. It will also dictate your legacy to all those whom you have loved and nurtured in your lifetime. The answer will determine who will follow in your footsteps and the wider impact your life will have had.

For Pilate, the answer is vague and uncertain: "Am I a Jew?" He is saying, "I have no idea! I have just heard the rumours."

The Kingdom is Here[246]

Jesus always points to the Father. He is the way (and the truth and the life) to the Father.[247] Jesus' whole mandate is to bring the Kingdom and reign of God back to earth. For now, at this moment as He has this famous discourse with Pilate, the Kingdom has not yet been unleashed on the face of the earth.

It is still a heavenly Kingdom. It waits for the redemption of humanity. It will find its expression through the Church and will begin its evangelistic tsunami in just a few short weeks' time when the Holy Spirit is poured out upon the fledgling believers.

Pilate recognises this Kingdom. "You're a king!" The Gospel writers have included this as a question in their recollections. John sees it as a statement: *you are!*

Jesus knew His purpose, the reason He was born: to testify to the truth that the Kingdom of Father God had to be established. For that to happen everything had to be reset on earth. The image of humanity. The nature of God's love; not that His love had ever changed for Jesus' coming proves that, but its nature had been lost to humankind. The price for sin had to be paid, the lost sought, blind healed, mute speak and dead raised. Jesus was literally opening the door to the Kingdom.

Knowing your purpose and living your purpose are two very different things. Unless you know why you are born – not just generic reasons, to worship God and win the lost, but your individual purpose – you will have a frustrated life. You will spend your time chasing at something that is out of your grasp. The false assumption here is that people must be educated regarding their reason for being.

---

[246] John 18:35-38.
[247] John 14:6.

Education and study are important for they show that you are purposeful about your purpose! However, something deeper is needed. You need to recognise the individual calling you have, your heavenly appointment, and to move in that daily. For this you may have to add study. The diligence of your study will show godliness and the calling you have.[248] The effort you put into your call will lead you into being the called.

Jesus understood His reason for being:

> *"...for this reason I was born, and for this I came into the world."*[249]

Everyone has spent a roughly equivalent time in their mother's womb prior to birth. That's a physical act that cannot be disputed. The reason you were born into this world was to find salvation through Jesus Christ, to worship Father and to lead others to Him. That is the role of those who are born again only. The unsaved cannot lead the unsaved to salvation. God's purpose is that everyone will be saved through Jesus, that none will perish.[250] You are born longing for more, to know why you are here and what you are made for. Every precious baby has to have the opportunity to meet with Jesus during their lifetime. It is the reason for the miracle of your existence.

Jesus knew there was more to living than just to be born – "...and for this I came into the world." He understood why He had been sent and what He was to do. He was not simply born with a purpose, His being *was* the purpose. He fulfilled His purpose.

It is vital to fulfil the purposes of God in your life, in your generation.[251] That means you have to move from a generic call on your life – the core reason for being alive in Christ – to the specific reason for being. That does not always mean so-called 'full-time Christian ministry'. There are those who will be involved in this in their lives and they should serve there well, with integrity. There is a myriad of calls: parenting, being a spouse, careers, volunteering, charitable roles, medical works, business, entrepreneurship. All of

[248] 2 Timothy 2:15 (NKJV).
[249] John 18:38.
[250] 2 Peter 2:3.
[251] Acts 13:36.

these and more can be Kingdom calls and preachers should never, never make such people feel that they have taken a lesser role.

How do you fulfil the purposes of God in the home and the workplace? By being salty, bright and fruitful.[252] How do you become those things in the workplace, in your life, in your very being? By spending time with God, praying, drawing closer to Jesus through reading the Word and being filled with the Holy Spirit. It's what used to called a 'quiet time' in Christian parlance.

"Impossible!" I hear you protest. "My life is so busy I cannot fit another thing in."

Let me ask a question: why would having a quiet time – just, say, fifteen minutes each day – be so resisted by the enemy of your soul? Why would the devil resist this so much, this little segment of the day?

Because it is the power station in life.

I know it's not easy. Perhaps the reason Christians feel downtrodden and ignored for their faith by others is because the saltiness is lost and, according to Jesus, salt-less salt is good only for being trampled underfoot. There's hope though! There is the possibility of change, to reclaim your purpose, your reason for being, to produce fruit that will outlive you; to leave a legacy. It all starts with that quiet time. It's vital to regain your first love.[253] For wherever you are, whatever your role or position in life, His Kingdom has come there because you are there.

Truth!

Pilate is a man who is used to lying to keep his position. He has lost sight of what is truly right or wrong. His now famous question to Jesus is echoed in our generation:

> *"What is truth?"*[254]

Truth has become so subjective today that it is hard to identify. So many things compete as being true that you have been encouraged by culture to believe that lies are also true. All this is very subtle and not

---

252 Matthew 5:13-16; John 15:16.
253 Revelation 2:4.
254 John 18:37b-38.

always obvious. Therefore, when Christians voice an opinion that is biblical, they will be called radicals, bigots, judgmental and intolerant. 'Tolerance' is a word now used to describe all behaviours as sin-free, all lifestyles as equal, all relationships as the same. All this is to knock at the door of ever-increasing liberalism in a world that has lost its way. Truth has to be true and if something else stands up and claims to be true, being opposite to actual truth, then it must be false.

Jesus says He is here to testify to the truth. Not *a* truth. *The* truth. That means there is no higher fact in history or the future that will ever override it, dilute it or render it meaningless. It stands alone and for eternity as a beacon to draw humankind's attention into its light. It is the one thing people have to find to satisfy the yearnings of their soul. That truth is encapsulated in one beautiful word, a name of such overwhelming power that all demons shudder at its mention and all unrepentant sinners will one day quake: *Jesus.*

This is the third truth statement Jesus makes in John's Gospel.[255] Jesus has said two empathic things about the truth in the Gospel already:

> *"Then you will know the truth, and the truth will set you free."*
>
> *"I am the way and the truth and the life. No one comes to the Father except through me."*[256]

Jesus is saying to Pilate, "I have come to change everything, for I am the Truth, I am the One who will bring rest to weary souls like yours, I am the one who will exonerate humanity."

Pilate misses the clue, and simply remarks, "What is truth?" because he has lived a life that is pulled in so many directions, keeping so many happy, trying to maintain a status quo, that he finds himself in another situation where there will be a loser; he just does not want it to be him. He is a man out of his depth.

---

[255] There are many references where Jesus says, "I tell you the truth," or in the KJV, "Verily, verily I say unto you." These are truth statements that point to the truth of who He is, Kingdom truths. In that sense they are subordinate truths to the Truth, who is Jesus, for they only find their reality in His existence and will.

[256] John 8:32, 14:6.

It is clear to Pilate that Jesus is no criminal; a sage maybe, a king definitely, for He speaks as one with authority. He declares Him innocent. There is no criminal charge that can be laid against Him!

That should be the end of this matter. It isn't.

In the mix of all of this the priests and people declare that they have no king but Caesar. This is more than just forcing Pilate's hand, for if he does not acquiesce and crucify Jesus, the people can claim that Pilate has a king other than Caesar. There is also a spiritual truth at work here: there will always be an allegiance to a ruling authority, even if that authority presents itself as anarchy. Independence and autonomy are illusions in the world. When the people declare that they are under Caesar's rule they effectively shun Yahweh. Everyone is under the influence of something or someone. No exceptions. If they had paused to reflect they may have realised that this was actually the consequence of their rash fervour. When people reject Jesus, they reject God too.

Son of God

Pilate seems intent on releasing Jesus. He is a man in a very deep hole and needs a plan. News about how he has governed is reaching Rome and the fact that he has executed innocent men under dubious circumstances. He needs a legitimate reason to release Jesus. The situation is unwinding in front of him all the time.

Enter Barabbas. This could be a solution. He has one of the most notorious criminals in the cells awaiting crucifixion. He is a murderer and an insurrectionist. Barabbas has killed his own people. It has become Pilate's custom to release a prisoner chosen by the people at their Passover Feast, a way of showing goodwill and clemency. Having Barabbas brought before the crowd and the priests he offers an exchange; a reasonable person would leap at the chance of releasing Jesus. Surely they would not want Barabbas? The question is simple: "Do you want Barabbas or Jesus, called the Christ?" Pilate knows they are jealous of Jesus and his following. He is well aware too that he is called Messiah[257] by many and so uses Jesus' title.

There is a nuance of language here. Barabbas means 'son of Abba', or 'son of God'. The question is, really, do you want *a* son of

---

[257] Christ

God or *the* Son of God? The imagery here is powerful. Barabbas may have been named by his parents after a male in the family, possibly his father, although it is unlikely. A quick scan of the book of Numbers will show family lineage denoted with the precursor *bar,* meaning 'son of'. It would have been a bit odd to Jewish ears for a male child to be named God's son, for they were all God's children. Literally his name meant 'son of daddy', a familiar term not always associated with God by the Jews, but many would have understood the nuance. Christians' understanding of this is based on Romans 8:15, which says God's people cry out to Him as Abba. The contrast is striking between Jesus and Barabbas. There would have been some deliberation; a time-lapse for the priests to get around the crowds and have them cry out for Barabbas. There is a hiatus in the proceedings as Pilate sits on his throne.

A Bad Day Gets Worse

Ever had one of those days when nothing goes right? Pilate is certainly in the middle of one right now. As he awaits the answer from the crowd he feels a nudge at his elbow. It's a messenger, his wife's servant. She has never been one to interfere in matters of State, but there must be some urgent domestic matter for her to interrupt proceeding in this way. He ushers the servant away as he unfolds the note.

Time stands still. The world begins to spin. Her note tells him what he already knows: Jesus is innocent.[258] Now his wife is troubling him. This is no longer just a State matter. If it is not bad enough that he is trying to keep his place in the hierarchy, with his career on the wane, now he will have to explain his actions to his wife later on! She is his closest confidant, his one true friend when others around him are only interested in favours and the superficialities of political bargaining. Her interest in him is genuine. She would only interrupt if it were urgent. Breaking protocol in this way would be unwarranted otherwise. For a superstitious woman, and possibly an equally

---

[258] Matthew 27:19b. We often assume that it was the Holy Spirit who troubled her so. This is not clear in Scripture. Certainly Pilate would not jump to that very Christian conclusion. He would think it was one of the Roman gods, perhaps his own personal one he worshipped.

superstitious Pilate, things were rapidly escalating out of control. Another way would need to be found.

Punishing the Innocent[259]

Pilate has no real desire to release a despicable criminal back on the streets. Jesus, in his view, is harmless to the Roman cause; His Kingdom is not even here on earth! He sends Jesus to be flogged.

Jesus' suffering was total and complete. Flogging was for lesser crimes though too, although often used as a precursor to crucifixion. Jesus was already bruised by the Sanhedrin. He had been punished by the religious court, though they were driving for more. He had to be found guilty by a criminal court too. Jesus had to die for *all* sins, not just those of a religious nature. The extent of the flogging depended entirely upon the mood and nature of the soldiers carrying it out. Perhaps they were stirred by the crowd. Perhaps they were eager for a chance to humiliate the accused. Part of flogging was a taunting, abusive name-calling and ridicule. They formed a crown of thorns and rammed it upon Jesus' head. They punched Him after the flogging. His body would be entering into shock through the blood-loss He was now experiencing from the merciless flogging.

Here He Is!

Jesus is returned to Pilate. Pilate seems to be a man of pithy one-liners that have become the subject of sermons throughout the years. Here is another: "Here is the man!"[260] Other versions have "Behold the man!"

Two things are happening here. Pilate is attempting a last gasp plea as if to say, "See, I have punished Him. He has learnt His lesson!" This does not satisfy the now hysterical crowd. The priests have done their job well. There is no stopping this frenzied juggernaut. Pilate is also actually identifying Jesus to them, for He is already very disfigured from a bout of punches from the Sanhedrin, a flogging, another beating from the soldiers who knew how to hit and a crown of thorns. The bruising, open wounds and blood pouring

[259] John 19:1-16.
[260] John 19:6.

down over His face would have disguised Jesus' identity. Pilate is literally saying, "It's really Him!" so shocking was his appearance.

"CRUCIFY, CRUCIFY!"

Pilate is now running scared. The priests press on and cite their law; Jesus has claimed to be God's Son.

The Power of Life and Death[261]

God is in control. He always has been. He holds the power of life and death, numbering your days, ordaining them.[262] Pilate begins to assert his authority in the matter and presses Jesus on this issue. Jesus has gone back to silence, standing before Pilate, dripping blood on the floor after a devastating flogging. Pilate asserts he has the power of life and death over Jesus.

Jesus does something radically unusual here. He firstly acknowledges Pilate's power. When someone has authority over you, whether they yield it benevolently or cruelly, you have to acknowledge they actually have that authority. It must be respected, even if the person in the position of power is a numpty. 'Numpty' is a useful word, a Scottish slang word, meaning someone who (sometimes unwittingly) by speech or action demonstrates a lack of knowledge or misconception of a particular subject or situation to the amusement of others.[263] Jesus may be amused but He does not show it. He acknowledges the truth of what Pilate has said: he does have authority and power. This must have been surprising for Pilate who is living in a time when his position is threatened.

Jesus acknowledges the source of the authority too. All authority comes from God. He is omnipotent. Jesus is basically saying, "Pilate, you have power, but only to the extent that my Father wills it." This is amazing. Jesus is weakened from His beatings and scourging, yet still acknowledges God's hand at work in His life. How often do you, in the midst of pain and suffering, turn your back on God? Some claim everything that happens is from the devil if it does not seem to carry a persona of blessing with it. This kind of superficial attitude to

---

[261] John 19:10-11.

[262] Psalm 139:16.

[263] http://www.urbandictionary.com/define.php?term=Numpty; accessed 30/12/15.

life and faith is abhorrent to me. I do not like suffering any more than the next person. I have had my fair share of heartache and trials in my life, some of my own making, some at the hands of others. I know that there are many people who have suffered far more than I have. There are those who are dying today for their faith as I write in a place of comfort. In the Western Church we have forgotten that suffering has always been part of the Christian experience. The flabby gospel of comfort would be a foreign thing to many brothers and sisters around the world. Jesus, dizzy with blood-loss and in physiological shock, knowing these are His last hours on earth, gives honour to God. Do the same, even in less trying situations.

Jesus acknowledges Pilate's sin and how it fits into the framework of the events of the day: "Yes, Pilate, you are committing a sin, about to hand over an innocent man to be executed, but those who have handed me over to you have committed the greater sin."

People will commit sins. Some sins are committed in ignorance, some are deliberate and planned, but they are still sins. Pilate's sin falls into the 'ignorant' category. He has no background knowledge, he is indecisive in this matter and is lost, grasping for an earthly solution. In so doing he will sin. He will hand Jesus over to be killed. His own soldiers will administer this death penalty. That's a pretty bad sin, wouldn't you agree?

Sin will condemn everyone to an eternity without God, in hell eventually, as unpopular as that thought has become.[264] Jesus grades sin though; one sin is greater than another. Those who have handed Him to Pilate have committed the greater sin. By implication, this means that different sins will carry different punishments, or levels of hell. Faithful service for the Lord brings all into the Father's rest.[265] There will also be levels of heaven; there will be greater rewards, positions, authority for those whose service and love for Jesus has been particularly exemplary.[266] What is true in the heavenly dimension will also be mirrored in the hellish one. Without repenting

[264] Romans 3:23.

[265] Matthew 25:21-23.

[266] Mark 10:25-40 makes it clear that there are places of greater reward in heaven which have been prepared for some people. Conversely, 1 Corinthians 3:10-15 suggests that there are those in heaven who got there by the skin of their teeth!

and accepting Jesus Christ as Lord and Saviour, a person will be condemned to their fate. Jesus even goes as far as to describe a hellish punishment on one occasion for those who sin against children.[267]

A person with a predisposition towards judgement, not mercy, might be quite pleased about this. They might envisage that there are people who definitely should go to hell and have no chance of reprieve. However, God is just. He always does the right thing even if the right thing is forgiving someone.[268] If you think that you cannot follow Jesus because there are some people who should never be forgiven their sins, remember: He forgave *you.* You may not have been an axe murderer or a Pontius Pilate, but all sin means God's standard is missed. You cannot plead mercy for yourself and then judgement for others. God fully appreciates the value of forgiveness and the preciousness of everyone's soul.

Standing before Pilate, Jesus soothes the distressed Roman governor with beautiful words of forgiveness: "There are those worse than you, Pilate." It's as though Jesus is putting Pilate's sin into context – as He does with you and me, for He understands our weaknesses yet is without sin – and allows Pilate the freedom to choose whom he will serve.[269] Pilate chooses to ignore the offer. He chooses the weak man's way.

Hand Jive![270]

It is not clear if the washing of hands in public was a traditional ritual for a Roman governor. Pilate wants everyone to know that he is not guilty of the crucifixion that is about to happen. He has bowed to pressure and fears that the news of this will get back to Rome.[271] So Pilate calls for water and washes his hands, as if that would make him truly clean. Yes, it is symbolism, but it symbolises the wrong thing. Pilate is demonstrating that he can, even symbolically, exonerate himself from the crime that is about to be committed. He has his wife's advice whirling in his mind, the ongoing onslaught of

---

[267] Matthew 18:6.
[268] Matthew 7:21-23.
[269] Hebrews 4:15.
[270] Matthew 27:11-26.
[271] John 19:12.

verbal abuse and the fear of a riot from the Jews assembled before him, and the compassionate and forgiving bruised eyes of an innocent man watching him. He caves in.

Earlier we saw how Adam and Eve tried something similar. They made coverings for themselves and stood in the presence of Father God. In His compassion He made them new coverings from animal skins for there can be no forgiveness without the shedding of blood.[272] Now Pilate is doing the same thing. He is trying to expunge shame and guilt by his own means whilst standing in the presence of Holy God, whose blood is about to be shed for the sins of the world, including his.

Trying to forget the bad you have done in your life is worthless. Time may numb the memory somewhat but you are still guilty. The phrase, "I wash my hands of this," is taken directly from this biblical account. There is a problem: it just does not work.

There is an old phrase heard across the years in the Church: "Are you washed in the blood?"[273] It's a great question but because it sounds gory and the imagery is unpleasant; it's fallen into disuse. Forgiveness has been made easy and grace cheap. Yet eternal life came at great cost. It may be free for us at the point of delivery, but each time the sinner repents, the blood of Jesus pays the price.

When self-cleansing from sin is tried there is a stench left behind; it lingers. On vacation in Spain my wife had heard about mud baths where you could go and smother yourself in silt from the seabed. Being a dutiful and loving husband, I agreed to go along. We arrived and found that these baths were actually a mini-lagoon that had been created to stop the precious sludge from escaping into the Mediterranean. Locals believe that there is great medicinal benefit in the mud and that after many applications, various ailments will improve. Jetties and ramps had been built to help people get into the waist-high water. Then it was a question of scraping along the lagoon bed with a container to get some gloop. Once we had got the precious gooey substance we made our way back to the jetty and began the process of covering ourselves with this natural exfoliate. There were a couple of things we were not told about. There are a lot of shells, grit

---

272 Hebrews 9:22.
273 Revelation 7:14.

and, at that time of year, tadpoles in the mud. It was literally mud with little eyeballs! It also has a strong sulphuric aroma. It was like Lazarus after four days in the tomb: it stinketh! We, being good tourists, waited for the mud to dry and harden until we looked like we had the skins of grey rhinoceroses, and then went back into the water to wash it off. That's where things got interesting. It was not that easy. Sure, the main areas of backs and legs cleaned off pretty quickly, but the water was getting muddier by the second as we washed and further disturbed the mud underfoot. We were literally cleaning ourselves with dirty water. Under our fingernails and between our toes was a challenge. Eventually we felt we had achieved a certain level of cleanliness and got out and dried ourselves. Being late in the day we headed off back to our apartment. My wife was so excited at how soft her skin was. I was so excited about the lovely shower waiting for me! Nonetheless, after the shower – and I had scrubbed properly – I could still smell the sulphur. In fact, it remained for a few days.

Trying to wash away your own sins is like trying to wash stinking mud off in putrefied water. You may get the mud off visually but you will still smell. The Psalmist uses the same illustration:

> *He lifted me out of the slimy pit, out of the mud and mire; he set my feet on a rock and gave me a firm place to stand.*[274]

The King James Version, and some others, refer to this as "miry clay". It's clay or mud that sticks, that is slippery and makes your footing unsure. You will always carry the aroma of where you have been. It's true of sin and it's true of the presence of God. If You spend time with Him you will find you have the aroma and fragrance of heaven about you.[275]

Pilate, still reeking of his sin, hands Jesus over to be crucified. He is not innocent; he is guilty of executing an innocent man. He knows it, symbolism or not. Jesus knows it. The crowds know it. Pretending it is otherwise does not help. He has clean hands but a dirty heart.

---

[274] Psalm 40:2.

[275] 2 Corinthians 2:15.

Pilate's Unhappy Ending

After attacking the Samaritans on Mount Gerizim around 36 A.D., Pilate was reported to Vitellius, legate of Syria, whereupon he was ordered back to Rome to stand trial for acts of cruelty and particularly the accusation that he executed men without proper trial. He had shed many innocent men's blood. Without his political benefactor he was totally exposed. According to Eusebius of Caesarea's Ecclesiastical History, Pilate killed himself on orders from Emperor Caligula in 39 A.D.

It would seem that as cruel as the Romans could be to those they suppressed, they would not tolerate what they saw as injustice. Pilate was ultimately a soldier and found himself outmanoeuvred politically by those who wanted him ousted.[276] Potentially he lost his life for killing Jesus, an innocent man.

---

276 http://www.britannica.com/biography/Pontius-PilatePage, accessed 30/12/15.

CHAPTER SEVENTEEN

Simon's Story

Simon's story can be read in Matthew 27:32, Mark 15:21 and Luke 23:26.

Cyrene is located on the continent of Africa in what is now Libya, about nine hundred miles away from Jerusalem, a journey of several weeks for Simon. Most likely a Jew coming to celebrate Passover, this could have been part of an annual pilgrimage for him. There was a known Jewish community in Cyrene some three hundred years before Christ's death. The Cyrenian Jews had their own synagogue.[277] Some of them were present when Peter preached his first sermon.[278]

Three Gospels recount that Jesus did not carry the cross – probably the crossbeam rather than the upright as well – but as they were led towards Golgotha, Simon was forced to carry the cross. Luke actually tells us he carried it behind Jesus. Given the physical torture He had already endured it should not be surprising that Jesus was beyond exhaustion. He had sweated blood, been beaten, scourged, and had a crown of thorns rammed upon his head.[279] He had already endured more than most could have hoped to survive.

---

277 Acts 6:9.

278 Acts 2:10; see also Acts 11:20 and 13:1. For further references to this people group see http://www.hprweb.com/2014/04/carrying-the-cross-with-simon-of-cyrene/, accessed 27/07/15.

279 Luke 22:44; John 18:22-23; Mark 14:65; Matthew 27:26,29-31

Who Is He?

It had been a long trip and had taken them several weeks. The journey from Cyrene was tiring but he wanted his sons, Alexander and Rufus, to experience a Passover in their spiritual home Jerusalem. They had travelled with others from the Synagogue for safety's sake. The Jewish community had been meeting together in Cyrene for centuries and the annual pilgrimage was part of their tradition. His sons were excited. They were now old enough to make the trip and were considered teen-men, having come of age.[280]

Jerusalem was a busy place at Passover. There seemed to be heightened tensions about the place. Rumours were circulating that a religious teacher had been on trial. Simon had never heard of this Jesus but from what he learnt that day He sounded like a renegade: breaking Sabbath laws, claiming to be God, even using the power of the devil to heal people. He wanted nothing to do with Him.

People were lining the street. The trial was over and there was to be a crucifixion. Simon, more out of curiosity than real interest, stood at the road side near the Praetorium, just along from the Governor's Palace. He had no desire to make his way to Golgotha as so many did, to actually witness the torturous death of the convicted, but observing from a safe distance was something he could do. He had never actually seen a crucifixion. He had seen corpses on crude crosses – most people in Roman occupied territories had; they were a regular reminder not to fall foul of their oppressors. He had no desire to expose himself or his sons to the unrestrained brutality of an actual crucifixion. One day their promised Messiah would come and bring the freedom they so craved. For now, he pitied these criminals but felt they deserved their fate if they had antagonised the Romans. It was hard enough in Cyrene to keep your head down, but he knew of many in Jerusalem who worked subversively against their oppressors.

There was a commotion which brought Simon's attention back to the present. People were crowding in, shouting abuses as three men carried the cross beams of their doom. Roman guards pushed the crowds back, keeping a narrow pathway for those on their final walk to make their way down. One seemed to be shouting back at the

---

[280] See note (v) in 'Additional Notes' on page 241.

crowd. He seemed to be mocking them. Another seemed detached, weeping, pleading for mercy with his expression. The third took Simon's breath away. He was wearing a crown crudely fashioned from thorns. He was bloodied and beaten, his clothes crimson from an obvious flogging. This was unusually cruel even for the Romans. Most would die eventually from such wounds.

Simon looked away, trying to leave, repulsed by what he was witnessing, but the crowds seemed to hold him there. They shouted abuse at this most tortured one, stirred on by their religious fervour.

Thud! Simon looked. Stumbling, one had crashed to the ground, the weight of the cross tearing at His already shredded flesh. Jesus had fallen at his feet, the crossbeam pinning Him to the floor. The Roman guard was shouting at Him, whipping Jesus again across his shoulders: "Get up, scum. Move!" He struggled but blood loss and exhaustion had overtaken Him. There was no way He was moving.

Simon felt the rough, vice-like grip on his coat pulling him forward before he realised what was happening, "You! Carry the cross for him! Walk behind him." He started to object but could see the look in the eye and a hand move towards a sword.

Simon raised his hands in surrender and knelt down beside the fallen man. Releasing the ropes that had been tied round the wrists of Jesus, he was conscious of just how much blood there was. He tried not to look at his face, but their eyes met.

The world fell silent around them.

Simon was expecting a plea from him, for help, or even vehemence. Instead Jesus looked into his eyes and Simon's heart melted. For there, through a face barely recognisable as being a man, through swollen eyes, broken teeth and a swollen and bloodied face where there had once been a beard, were eyes of warmth and tenderness.[281] Eyes that showed pity and compassion for Simon. Innocent eyes. A look that stirred something in his heart, reminding him of something he had heard read many times and had committed to memory long ago: "He was oppressed and afflicted, yet he did not open his mouth; he was led like a lamb to the slaughter, and as a sheep before its shearers is silent, so he did not open his mouth."[282]

---

281 Isaiah 53:3b.
282 Isaiah 53:7.

The guard was shouting, "Pick it up; get moving!"

Simon lifted the burden on to his shoulder. It was heavy; no wonder Jesus had stumbled. Slowly, Jesus rose to His feet. He looked at Simon once more, an enigmatic look that told Simon in an instant that this was for him. He turned and walked on, Simon the pilgrim walking behind Him on the way to Golgotha. A mile to walk carrying a cross.

He had walked some nine hundred miles to Jerusalem. He was now walking the first mile as a new follower of Jesus. Every abusive expletive that was hurled at Jesus took on a new meaning for Simon as he realised these were taken for him. Occasionally people would step into the road and slap Jesus or spit on Him. No retaliation or words came from Him though. Just love. Occasionally Simon would shift the weight of the gnarled wood as the beam would bear down upon him.

When they reached the dreadful place, the soldiers pointed to where they wanted it lain. Releasing the burden, he realised his cloak had stuck to it for there was fresh blood, Jesus' blood, tacky and still sticky and now marking his tunic.

He looked once more at Jesus who was standing unsteadily, waiting for the soldiers to make their preparations, surveying the crowds who had gathered. Their eyes met one last time as the centurion pushed Simon backwards into the crowds.

His sons. Where were his sons? He looked around. They were pushing their way forward. Tears were streaming down crimson cheeks. They hugged. They were fearful. He reassured them and told them he was alright. Then they turned and looked. By now Jesus was on the cross looking down upon them all.

The three of them would never be the same.

Perhaps they stayed on in Jerusalem to do some trading and to celebrate Shavuot, the Feast of Weeks. During this time, it is possible they met other followers of Jesus, hearing that He had been raised from the dead. They may even have been present amongst five hundred others on one occasion when He appeared.[283] They eventually returned home.

Changed men. Committed men. Spirit-filled men!

---

[283] 1 Corinthians 15:6.

A new Christian community soon sprang up in Cyrene alongside the synagogue and gained in popularity. Rufus, one of Simon's sons, became its leader. Paul, the great preacher, became a close family friend, always enjoying the hospitality Simon's wife showed.[284]

Something life-transforming happens when the cross is encountered. The imagery of Simon carrying the cross behind Jesus is symbolic. It reminds everyone that they are the ones worthy of God's wrath, for they are the transgressors, not Jesus. The moment when Simon lays down the crossbeam and Jesus is nailed to it is a powerful image. Jesus literally takes your place.

Theologians call this penal substitution, where Jesus took your punishment as your substitute. This realisation means you can never truly be the same again. Simon walked a mile behind Jesus, following a blood trail that led to a new place of covenant between him and God. In the same way, you may find that you too walked in the bloodstained footprints of the Lamb, before committing to follow Him beyond the cross.

Many will enquire about who Jesus is and what He has done. It is when they reach the cross itself that they realise this is 'do or die'. The stumbling block is placed before them and they recognise that this moment will change them forever.[285] To follow Jesus to the cross is one thing; it is entirely another to follow Him beyond the cross.

It is interesting that no more is heard about Simon than in the Gospel accounts. One of his sons is mentioned alongside Simon's wife though. It is a postscript to the churches in the Roman empire. It is often in the postscripts that hope is gained. When a man comes to faith, when the family see the changes in that man, the family will follow. No doubt the events at Golgotha had a profound effect on young Rufus too. No doubt he made his own commitment as did his mother. All of that would have been in the wake of a transformed father and husband.

If you are a man reading this then give your life again to Jesus. Do not waste any more precious moments. Go beyond the cross with Him and discover that He is the best friend you will ever know and the only man you can emulate wholeheartedly. If you are a wife and

---

[284] Romans 16:13.
[285] 1 Peter 2:8.

your husband is not yet saved then do not give up hope. Accept that he will, like Simon, have to walk behind Jesus on the road to Golgotha carrying the cross. Accept, too, that he will stumble along that journey, for that road is uneven and full of detractors and those who would question why he is doing it. Recognize that there will be a point where he will have to accept or reject Jesus as he gazes fully into the magnitude of what has been done for him as a man.

CHAPTER EIGHTEEN

A Centurion's Story

This was not his first rodeo. He had been to many executions, performing them as a soldier. At least now, as a centurion, he could avoid the bloodlust. He could watch from a distance.

They led the three convicts through the mile-long walk to Golgotha; the armpit of the city, beyond which was the rubbish tip. All manner of garbage would be added daily to it, but today, for three criminals, it would be the last thing they would see. He had heard there was some urgency about this particular crucifixion, something about the locals having a feast of some description, so things had to be hurried up. His soldiers were doing their job, ushering them along.

There had been a short holdup as one of them had stumbled. The crossbeams were not light, and by the look of him the soldiers had gone to town with their flogging. A flogging before a crucifixion was not unusual. Normally it was enough to weaken a person, but not too much. There was an art to it; they did not want the criminal to die before they got them on to their cross. That would deny the right of the victims of whatever the crime was to hurl their abuse, sometimes their stones or rotting food, and that would be bad form. He would have to instruct the troops again; allowing their desire to maim to get the better of them was ill-disciplined.

He was impressed this man could walk at all. His minions had quickly and efficiently conscripted a passer-by to carry the crossbeam after Him. The man had looked terrified. Perhaps he thought he would end up crucified instead.

He marched on to the spot. His men knew the drill and lined up the condemned, stripping them all naked[286] before lying them on their crossbeams which were now slotted into their uprights.

He watched the crowd in his peripheral vision. Sometimes people would run forward to either kick the death row prisoner, or to try a last ditch attempt to free them. No one was that adventurous today. The normal struggles went on. He had seen it all. It was instinct to resist the outstretching of the arm as a nail was prepared. Normally it took two soldiers, one pulling on the arm, sometimes dislocating it at the shoulder, and one to hammer the six-inch iron spike through the wrist. Blood would gush forth initially as the radial or ulnar artery was crushed, depending on the accuracy of the hammer-wielder and the fight the convict put up. Ideally, dead centre of the wrist was best, trying to avoid both arteries; less blood spatter. Either way, as the spike was driven home it would crush and sometimes plug a nicked artery but invariably the ulnar nerve was crushed, which was excruciatingly painful, sending shockwaves up the arm, through the shoulder and to the base of the neck where the nerves split off on their journey from the brain.

Something caught his eye. The one who had fallen did not resist. Initially the centurion thought it was through weakness and resignation. No, it was not his imagination. He had laid Himself on the cross. No fighting or last ditch struggle. He refused the sour wine and gall,[287] the anaesthetic poison that would dull the pain but hasten death. Everyone took it. Senseless not to. Why experience all the pain? Then He had laid His own hands outstretched, looking into the eye of the nail bearer, nodding slightly as if to say, "I'm ready." The hammer had hesitated in the air a moment, as if the one striking were suddenly unsure.

---

286 Popular images and artworks of Jesus on the cross always depict Him as having a well-placed loincloth. This was more to do with protecting the more fragile in society from their blushes than actual truth. All those crucified were done so naked.

287 Matthew 27:33-34; Mark 15:23. See this simple explanation here: http://www.biblestudy.org/question/why-did-jesus-refuse-to-drink-wine-with-gall-whileon-cross.html, accessed 15/07/15.

He screamed like any other man as the blows hit: once, twice, three times. There were no expletives though. No cursing. Nothing. Just... just *empathy* in His bruised eyes.

They bent his legs, turning Him sideways at the waist and repeated the process with the nine-inch spike, straight through both ankle joints. The cross was then raised. The feet of the victim were only three or four feet from the ground.

Some objected to the charges listed above His head. It was the common practice to put these on the cross above the convicted to remind everyone of, firstly, how bad the person was and, secondly, to make sure others did not repeat their crimes. Pilate had sent along a board, with instructions to place it on the cross. That was unusual. Normally they would read the charge sheet and fabricate something themselves. This man must have some import. It read, "JESUS OF NAZARETH, KING OF THE JEWS," written in three languages: Aramaic, Latin and Greek.[288] The centurion was surprised by the anger shown by the chief priests, demanding he took it down. He refused. He was not about to get a ladder, climb up above the thorny crowned head of this man, and rewrite a sign. They stormed off to Pilate, but returned later, obviously having had no sway with the Governor.

Jesus had been tried before three courts: the religious court of the Sanhedrin; the cultural, local court of Herod; and the criminal court of Pilate. Now His status was declared in three languages: the historic and religious language of Aramaic; the judicial language of Rome, Latin; and the commercial, common language of Greek.

Jesus stood trial before all the courts and all the languages and cultures of the day in the Roman Empire, viewed as the whole world in those days. The sign on the cross was more than a statement. It had become the defining act of history – Jesus died to redeem all the justice systems in existence then and now. He died to redeem all cultures and all commerce too. All things are placed under His feet.[289] Therefore, for the born again Christian, there is nothing that is unspiritual, for as you walk in the footsteps of your Saviour you discover He has not just saved you but has redeemed your culture,

---

[288] John 19:19-22.
[289] Ephesians 1:22.

job and spirituality too. He provides true justice for you, called grace, where Jesus takes your punishment. There are immoral things and careers you should question your involvement in, for if nothing is unspiritual to Christians as an activity, then you need to weigh it morally. More than this though, because Jesus has redeemed commerce and culture, you become the change agent within these spheres as you seek to be salt and light.

The centurion stood at his post. His solders began to split up their spoils; a small perk of the job. A few coins here, a tunic there, but mostly the valuable possessions had been long since confiscated or stolen. The strange one had something of value. A robe. His soldiers drew lots for it. Too good a prize to tear equally, even though it was saturated with blood.[290]

He listened to the cries from the crosses. He saw how the strange one responded to the taunts of the one convict and the plea of the other. He saw Him speak to His mother and friend. He heard him pray. Heard Him forgive. Never had he seen such... such *grace.*

The sky grew dark, as though the sun had been cloaked, yet there was no visible storm or clouds. People screamed, crying out, for there were no flaming torches to give light at that hour. No one was prepared for darkness.[291] An omen, maybe, as though the light of the world had been extinguished.

Time was running out. They needed to hurry things along. Nodding to his sergeant, the men gleefully set about breaking the legs of two of the three. The shock, if they were still alive, would bring on cardiac arrest or suffocation as their lungs filled with fluid, as they could no longer lift themselves up against their nails to gasp for air. A soldier looked quizzically at the one in the middle. Dropping the club, he used his spear, forcing it just below the ribs towards the heart. A deft blow and one that he had used before. Blood and water flowed.[292] He had died some minutes before.

In his years the centurion had not seen anything like this. He had seen many protest against their crimes to the last breath. Death was not new to him; he had witnessed it many times on the battlefields as

---

[290] John 19:24.
[291] Luke 23:44.
[292] John 19:32-34.

Rome extended its empire and grip on those it subjugated. He had seen many die on a cross. However, he had never seen anyone die so... so *exquisitely;* as though they had the strength to overcome death and defy it, yet yielded to its grasp.

"Surely this was the Son of God,"[293] the centurion said in the darkness to no one in particular.

At that moment there was a warming in his heart. A stirring, an overwhelming peace. Although this man was innocent he understood He had to die. He looked up again at Him as the first Gentile convert.

People wanted His body. They came with instructions from Pilate himself.[294] Normally the bodies would be thrown over the cliff-face to rot on the rubbish after the birds had had their feed, as a reminder to all who would defy Rome. The orders, however, were clear. He allowed them. How could he refuse? They took his Saviour to be buried properly. It was the least he could do.

---

[293] Mark 15:39.
[294] Luke 23:52.

PART SIX

Words from the Cross

On the cross as He is dying Jesus is not silent. He says seven things. Some debate exists about the order in which these occurred but there is no debate that during His last few hours He did indeed say them. Speaking from the splayed position on the cross, with the weight of their body upon their arms, having to lift themselves up to catch a breath against the pain in the wrists and ankles, means any speech would have been difficult for those being crucified. We read the things Jesus said in the Bible as nice, clearly spoken phrases or sentences. In fact, these words of the cross were probably gasped, a few words at a time, after each exertion to capture the ever-evasive breath with which to speak.

CHAPTER NINETEEN

Forgiven!

"Father, forgive them; for they do not know what they are doing."[295]

Jesus' death was to allow access back to the Father. The blood of Jesus, shed on the cross, would pay the penalty for sin.

Some Christians seem to think that this was some kind of celestial bargain made with the devil, that in some way payment was given to him by Jesus' death. This is heresy and a misunderstanding of the need for God's wrath to be satisfied. Sin separated you from God. No other sacrifice could save you from the consequences of eternal separation from Him. God sent Jesus to die in your place and make the way open again back to the Father.[296]

There is something liberating in forgiveness and forgiving others. Without this vital ingredient life can become unbearable, hurts build up and, if sin remains unforgiven, judgment will surely come. The Bible warns the Christian not to harbour bitterness; it contaminates others around you and leads many into deception.[297] It needs to be dealt with.

Julie Andrews, in the musical 'Mary Poppins' sang, "A spoonful of sugar helps the medicine go down." The song refers to the potions available in those days that were often unpleasant to taste or bitter.

---

295 Luke 23:34.
296 Genesis 3:15; Colossians 1:19-20; 1 Peter 2:24; John14:6.
297 Hebrews 12:15.

Sugar is an antidote to bitterness. Forgiveness is the sweetness that God brings into your life to cancel out the bitter remains of unforgiveness.

True, I do not know what has happened to you in your life. You may have had it rough. If I knew what someone had done to you I too might be angry. It's okay to be angry. It's not okay to allow your anger to become sinful.[298]

What's the difference? Everyone gets angry. Even God.[299] Anger in itself is not sinful then. Some things you should be angry about: injustices, moral decay, the treatment of the marginalised. Be angry about the things that anger God. Rather than becoming pious and self-righteous as a result, become a proactive change agent who works for the causes of Father God. This is righteous anger.

Sinful anger is when your mood and rage are fed with resentment, embarrassment, unhealed wounds, criticism and plans for vengeance. These lead to bitterness. It locks a prison door over the heart with a sole inmate: you.

Christians are to display love and keep short accounts with others.[300] This unlocks the prison you place yourself in. It allows freedom to come. Forgiving others may not change the other person at all. They may not be aware that they have even wounded or offended you. Forgiving releases *you.*[301]

Unforgiveness and retaliation can be so ingrained that they become second nature, even when freedom is available. I once saw a documentary about a rhino that had been rescued as a young calf and raised in an enclosure on the edge of a game reserve. Each night it would go to sleep with the sounds of the animals of the bush. It grew smelling the aromas of its heritage. It lived within the promise of a great expanse to explore, but could not access this. It accepted this was its life. As it grew, the documentary chronicled how those caring for it intended to release it into the reservation. The time came to open the gate on the enclosure. You may think this now adolescent rhino bolted through the opening into its freedom. It didn't. It sniffed

---

298 Ephesians 4:26.
299 Exodus 4:14; Numbers 25:3 etc.
300 1 Corinthians 13:5.
301 R.T. Kendall has written extensively about this subject in *Total Forgiveness* and *Totally Forgiving Ourselves.*

a bit at the exit, but by and large ignored it. Gradually, the gate was left open for longer times. Eventually, after a week or so, they left the enclosure open permanently. It took days for the rhino to take its first tentative steps outside and then return. Little by little it would venture farther and farther into the reserve. Eventually, one day it left and never returned.

Jesus has opened a way for you to forgive others by Him forgiving you. The same forgiveness you have been shown by Him you are to show to others.[302] If you do not, it's like the rhino, once wounded but now healthy, choosing to remain in a small enclosure when freedom beckons.

When Jesus forgives from the cross, He is not just asking God to forgive those who have crucified Him, although that is obvious. He is demonstrating how forgiveness works. In the midst of His pain He cries out for those who have so mortally wounded Him. He intercedes for them. As He is dying, He mediates for them. It is the point of the cross. Without forgiveness the cross is just another instrument of torture devised by cruel people to be forgotten in the eons of history. With forgiveness it becomes the most powerfully recognisable of all symbols of Christendom. It stands for eternity as the moment when heaven was beckoned back to earth, in which Father's love could be lavishly restored to your soul, where the Father is invited to walk again with you. With forgiveness the whole world can know redemption. With forgiveness the possibilities are endless. The Son has made the way. The access to the Father is restored. Heaven beckons you to receive the open arms of Father's love. One thing, only one thing, needs to be done to experience it. One thing remains undone. One thing remains your remit to this great invitation: *repentance.*

Repentance opens up the riches of heaven to you. God's love is like a huge reservoir against a dam wall that is specifically designed to hold back the flow. Sin is that dam wall. Repentance – total, abandoned repentance – that throws itself into the arms of the Saviour obliterates it. As with any dam, the water will flood and destroy whatever is in its path with unstoppable force. Repentance brings that force of Father God's love back to you, erasing the past

302 Matthew 6:15.

and creating a new reality in the present and a different future. Without repentance, the cross is merely two wooden posts crudely nailed together by a carpenter two thousand years ago.

Repentance is more than a lifestyle choice. It is more than saying sorry. It is a very descriptive word, *metanoéo,* which is made up of two words meaning 'changed after being with' and 'think'; literally 'to think properly afterwards'.[303] After what? When you encounter Jesus on the cross it is more than a change of mind; it leads to change in thought, and a change in thought leads to a change in action. When Jesus is encountered, His plea interceding for your forgiveness on the cross, indifference cannot be the response. Either a person is fully sold out for God or, deep in their heart, they decide to walk on past Him.

Rejection of Christ is not indifference. It is what Jesus called the unforgivable sin.[304] If you think you have committed it, the chances are you have not. Jesus' jibe was aimed at the Pharisees.

Without repentance forgiveness can never be enjoyed from the Father. People may find this unfair. Surely unforgiveness, and therefore judgement, is for really bad people: axe murderers, thieves, child abusers? Surely good people will get into heaven? There is only one good person in heaven: Jesus. Everyone else is there, or will go there, because of Him and their acceptance of Him as Saviour and Lord. Period. You may be good. You're probably better than me. You're not better than Him. He's the standard. He is the one who cries out to forgive you. You have to cry out to Him to receive that forgiveness. It's not rocket science. It is humbling. Admitting the need to be forgiven means seeing God as holy and offended by sin.

There is much written and preached today that proclaims a universalist gospel: everyone will get in because God's love is so great He could never allow anyone to go to an eternity without Him. It is proclaimed that salvation can happen after death. Whilst God's love is unfathomable, as Christ calls out from the cross, God's love is being clearly demonstrated and delivered to humanity. John 3:16 is being acted out before a fallen race. God's love is beyond measure. Beyond description, awesomely magnificent, that love searches out

303 http://biblehub.com/greek/3340.htm, *metanoéo,* accessed 31/12/15.
304 Matthew 12:22; Mark 3:29.

the sinner and beckons you into the new life on offer. It is a time-sensitive offer though. For as much as the grace passages of Scripture proclaim the incredible love of God, the justice verses of Scripture clearly state that this is a lifetime-only opportunity.[305] A gospel that ignores the justice of God is not really the gospel. It is not that people should be coerced into the church out of fear of judgment; they should be compelled by the love of God. Think about your salvation experience. Was it God's love or justice that brought you into His arms? My guess is it was His love. Fear is never a great motivator for anything. Why would it be different for any of your friends?

Right now is a time of grace; God has not judged the world yet. When Jesus reads from the scroll at the beginning of His ministry in Luke 4:18-19, He stops mid-verse. Okay, I know there were no numbered verses in the passage that He read from Isaiah.

He is reading from Isaiah 61:1-2. Go check it out. Notice anything? Jesus ends His reading, "To proclaim the year of the Lord's favour..." The passage in the Old Testament continues with, "...and the day of vengeance of our God." The world is in a grace space right now. Jesus has set up every opportunity to receive Him. Justice will be fulfilled too. As much as this may seem unpalatable to liberal scholars and fringe evangelicals, it's still the painful truth – one that I do not believe that God takes any pleasure in, but it is an action of His perfection and holiness. It seems that God is far more balanced in His love/justice theology than His Church can ever be. This realisation should propel our witness to new levels.

Forgiveness is available. Now.

[305] Hebrews 9:27; 2 Peter 2:9.

Chapter Twenty

Paradise Beckons

One of the criminals who hung there hurled insults at him: "Aren't you the Messiah? Save yourself and us!" But the other criminal rebuked him. "Don't you fear God," he said, "since you are under the same sentence? We are punished justly, for we are getting what our deeds deserve. But this man has done nothing wrong." Then he said, "Jesus, remember me when you come into your kingdom." Jesus answered him, "Truly I tell you, today you will be with me in paradise."[306]

During the torturous crucifixion many people hurled insults at Jesus. It was not uncommon for this to occur; people would read the inscription above the head of the dying criminal and berate them. Jesus was subjected to the rejection of His divinity by those who watched Him suffer.

In the midst of this there is a conversation between the three who hang before the crowd. One criminal decides to join in with the insults, but also to ask for his deliverance. *Save yourself; save us too!* You will hear this kind of entreaty all the time as people reject Jesus but want His intervention without His Lordship. They will say things like, "If He is really God then why did He let this bad thing happen to me?" or, "If He did not want this to happen, why didn't He intervene?" Many people are like this first criminal, not literally

---

[306] Luke 23:39-43.

hanging from a cross, but still nailed to the consequences of their actions. In those situations they ask for deliverance, not believing that it will actually materialise, with no intention of changing their lives and submitting to Christ's rule. The criminal, had Jesus indeed saved him from death there and then – and He could have done so – had no intention of changing his life. That is not repentance. Sometimes apologies are genuine and sometimes not. Sometimes a sorry is an apology for being caught, without any true change of heart. So this criminal joins in the mocking. Scorning others and deflecting attention from one's own sin does not make a person any less guilty. It might be an habitual defensive tactic, but it does not change the facts of the matter: they are still paying for their sin.

The second criminal is different. He rebukes the first through his own anguish. Perhaps they were partners in crime. He seems to know enough about the one who is verbally mocking Jesus to know he is worthy of death. He tells his friend to back off; they deserve their punishment, but Jesus, He is innocent! It is doubtful that they could all look at each other due to the contorted position they are all in, but they can hear each other. In faith, he says, "Remember me when you come into your kingdom."

It is not clear if he knew anything about Jesus before they met in this way – there is no other record of him in the Gospels – but it is likely he knew about Jesus and that He was a king. In the middle of trials and tribulations remember who the King is! Some things God will deliver you from. Some things He will sustain you through. Sometimes you will feel like part of you is dying. There are pains that you experience that are inexplicable. Your prayer and plea can only be, "Remember me!"

Jesus offers incredible words of comfort in the midst of His own pain. It was for this that He came, to save sinners, and there, as heaven holds its breath and creation sees its redemption drawing near, a sinner repents! There is an extraordinary moment in heaven at this point. There is anguish at what Jesus is suffering, however necessary, for the Radiance of heaven is dying. There is also celebration, for heaven always rejoices over even one sinner that repents.[307] Jesus does not just give words to comfort the soul, He

---

[307] Luke 15:7.

gives an unbreakable promise: "Truly I tell you, today you will be with me in paradise." He is saying, "Yes, today you will die. But you will also be with me in paradise!"

Heaven Can't Wait

Obviously Jesus is talking about heaven, right? At first glance it appears so. To understand what Jesus has actually promised here you need to get to grips with Jewish cosmology; what they actually understood about heaven and hell. In doing so you will grasp a new understanding of some puzzling verses in the Bible. Hang in there; it will be worth it!

Throughout the Old Testament the Hebrew name for the place of the dead is Hades, referred to as Sheol in the New Testament. The tendency is to think that this is actually hell because of the influence of Greek mythology and hit movies like Disney's animated classic *Aladdin.* Not so. It is a realm with two divisions: a place of blessing and a place of judgment.[308] The habitat of the saved and the lost are both generally called Hades in the Old Testament and Gospels. Therefore Hades cannot mean hell, for the holy do not go there. The two halves of Hades have different occupants. The place of the saved is often called 'Abraham's bosom' or 'Abraham's side' depending on the translation used. It is the place where the righteous Jew would desire to go to be with their patriarch, Abraham, a place that represented blessing and peace. It is also simply called 'paradise'.[309] When Jesus said to the repentant criminal he would be with Him in paradise that very day, He was talking about the paradise section of Hades, not heaven. Not yet.

The divides of Hades, where the righteous and evil go, are separated by a great chasm. No one can cross this. In Luke 16:19-31 Jesus tells the story of a rich man and a beggar called Lazarus. The rich man pleads for leniency and asks for a drink but he is refused because of the way he treated the poor man in his lifetime. He then pleads for Abraham to send Lazarus to his family to save them this future torment. Again, this is not acquiesced to for they have the

---

308 Matthew 11:23, 16:18; Luke 10:15, 16:23; Acts 2:27-31.
309 Luke 16:22, 23:43.

prophets. The point is, there are clearly two areas to Hades, which are not connected and cannot be cross-populated.

Jesus, when He died, went to this blessed side of Hades. After three days He was raised to life and at that point took all the inhabitants of the paradise section to heaven. This makes sense of the first strange verse you need to understand:

> *This is why it says: "When he ascended on high, he took many captives and gave gifts to his people." (What does "he ascended" mean except that he also descended to the lower, earthly regions? He who descended is the very one who ascended higher than all the heavens, in order to fill the whole universe.)* [310]

Notice the phrase "lower, earthly regions". It was believed that Hades is in the centre of the earth, not a different dimension or heaven beyond earth. Now here's the kicker. The judgment side of Sheol/Hades has remained unchanged. The unrighteous sinner still goes there, awaiting judgement. It's not limbo, but a real place of judgement, just not complete judgement yet. However, Jesus went there too.

There is a popular misconception that Jesus went to hell and preached there. Look at the second tricky passage:

> *For Christ also suffered once for sins, the righteous for the unrighteous, to bring you to God. He was put to death in the body but made alive in the Spirit. After being made alive, he went and made proclamation to the imprisoned spirits – to those who were disobedient long ago when God waited patiently in the days of Noah while the ark was being built.*[311]

Jesus died for the righteous and the unrighteous. He died for everyone. There were those who shunned God's prophets, their hope in Yahweh, and chose their own roads. Jesus, when He descended to Hades could cross the chasm for He is God. He is the only man who could. The judgement side of Hades is a place of torment. The

---

310 Ephesians 4:8-10.
311 1 Peter 3:18-20a.

torment was crystallised when Jesus walked through it showing the scars of the Lamb. This was not a cruelty. God is not vindictive. Yet they still had to see the promise of God fulfilled so that their rejection of God's love had meaning.

All unbelieving dead still go there awaiting their final judgment in the future. Hell, the lake of fire spoken of in Revelation,[312] is currently empty. It is a place reserved for final and future judgement, called the second death, not because there will be annihilation of the eternal souls of people, but because the judgement will be complete. When Christ ascended from Hades on resurrection Sunday things changed for the believer though. The paradise side of Hades is now empty, for because of Jesus' sacrifice and resurrection, you are now given instant access upon death into heaven.[313] Hades, then, is a place of the dead, for righteous and unrighteous, and at that moment when Jesus spoke from the cross, the godly dead were in a part of it too. He travelled with the now saved convict who died beside Him.

To Touch or Not to Touch? That is the Question!

This nuance in Scripture, which may have been new to you, helps make sense of another perplexing verse:

> *Jesus said, "Do not hold on to me, for I have not yet ascended to the Father. Go instead to my brothers and tell them, 'I am ascending to my Father and your Father, to my God and your God.'"*[314]

On the face of it this instruction to Mary seems odd because later Thomas is encouraged to touch Jesus.[315] There are some intricacies in the original text; there is a difference in the type of touch that was being given by Mary Magdalene. She grabs Jesus and clings to Him. She does not want to let Him go. Ever. Thomas' touch is a prodding, not a gripping, of Jesus.[316]

---

[312] Revelation 20:14-15.
[313] 2 Corinthians 5:8.
[314] John 20:17.
[315] John 20:27.
[316] http://www.gotquestions.org/touch-Mary-Thomas.html, accessed 08/10/15.

There is more to it than this though. I am sure that Jesus reciprocated the hug that Mary gave Him. I cannot imagine He would push her away. The clue is actually in the instructions to give to the disciples: "...for I have not yet ascended to the Father. ...tell them, 'I am ascending to my Father and your Father, to my God and your God.'" What is going on here? Remember, Jesus is bringing with Him all the righteous dead who believed before the crucifixion. Heaven is now open for business! Jesus has still to lead all these resurrected souls to heaven. He is going to present them to Father God, the first fruits of the resurrection. The welcome in heaven would have been extraordinary. Abraham, Moses, Elisha, Joshua, Caleb, David, Rahab, the heroes and the anonymous, entering into a new reality in the footsteps of Jesus as He boldly enters the throne room. The Trinity reunited. The roar of the trumpets, the songs of the angels, the joy of the Father!

Jesus still had some tasks to do on earth. He had to prepare the disciples for the next phase of the Kingdom. He returned to earth and walked among them. We tend to think that Jesus ascended to heaven just once because of the account in Acts 1:9 but the verse simply tells us this is the last time the disciples saw Him; he was hidden from them. It was not the first time He had ascended. As the perfect man, Jesus now had access to heaven whenever He chose, and also to earth.

The Gates of Hades

This basic understanding of Jewish cosmology helps to bring fresh insight to those occasions when Jesus had previously spoken about the gates of Hades. I often hear people saying the gates of hell will not overcome the Church, but this is a misquote of the Bible; Jesus says Hades.[317] What is Jesus telling His followers? When Jesus says "...the gates of Hades will not overcome it," He is proclaiming several things. Death and Hades will try to overcome the Church! They won't succeed. The gospel will be an anathema to those facing judgement but they will have no power. Whatever happens in this lifetime, even martyrdom, the Church wins! As the builder of the Church, Jesus is going to have to go there and prevail over death and

---

[317] Matthew 16:18.

Hades. He is going to release people into the presence of God. Heaven is real, for God will open up eternity to those who have already died, not just a place of temporary blessing. Judgement will come for those who reject God. There will always be a Church, for Hades represented death. The Church will never be extinguished. It may be persecuted, attacked, but never eradicated, for death does not win over the Christian individually nor corporately.

Hades was the most powerful thing people could think of at the time, an impenetrable prison only accessed by death; even this place could not overcome the Church.

Chapter Twenty-One

Family Matters

"Woman, behold, your son!" Then He said to the disciple, "Behold, your mother!"[318]

Theologians correctly assume that Joseph, Jesus' step-father, had died before His ministry. There is no mention of him in the Gospels after he and Mary return to Jerusalem after a pilgrimage to find their lost child. After that, nada, zip, silence. He was not present when Jesus' mother and family came looking for Him.[319] The reason why they come looking for Him is not clear in the narrative, but it is probably to do with the fact that Jesus would now have been regarded as the head of the household as the oldest living son of a deceased father.

In Mark chapter three, Jesus appears to snub His family. This is not the case. Mary, virgin-mother though she was, is not a perfect human with all of the information to hand. She has come looking for her son, along with his biological half-brothers, because Jesus should be taking care of them. He isn't. Not in the way that they understood, anyway. I am sure that He left enough money to tide them over. It is also probable that His younger brothers were also carpenters, and so there would be a steady income for the family. Incidentally, nowhere do we read that Jesus placed any financial charge or demand on the family business. His answer to those listening was that whoever does

[318] John 19:26-27.
[319] Mark 3:30-34.

the will of God are His family, His brothers and sisters and mother![320] Jesus is actually reminding them that this is why He came into the world in the first place, that there was a bigger plan at work.

The Gospels say that Jesus spoke to Mary, instructing her not to expose Him as a Messianic figure. It's a short conversation:

> *On the third day a wedding took place at Cana in Galilee. Jesus' mother was there, and Jesus and his disciples had also been invited to the wedding. When the wine was gone, Jesus' mother said to him, "They have no more wine." "Woman, why do you involve me?" Jesus replied. "My hour has not yet come." His mother said to the servants, "Do whatever he tells you."*[321]

Look at what Jesus actually says to her: "Woman, why do you involve me? My hour has not yet come." The footnote in my Bible reassures me that the term "woman" was not a derogatory term! *Phew!* The rest of the sentence, though, makes clear that Jesus was not too pleased to be asked to sort out the wine issue. I read this and I think there must have been a pretty determined quality about this woman! All the sermons I have heard about her portray her as a gentle, meek, innocent virgin with no life experience when she fell pregnant. She was those things, but under the surface there was also a gritty determination to get through the challenges of life. God chose well.

Mary goes to the servants, as if ignoring Jesus, and tells them to follow His instructions, pointing Him out to the group of waiters and saying, "Him! Do what He tells you to do!" These servants must have made their way to Jesus and just stood there, waiting for Him to give them instructions! Before you accuse me of claiming that Jesus was forced into this miracle, remember He tells a parable later about a persistent widow who kept bothering the judge all night until he acquiesced.[322] It seems Jesus pictured a God who likes earnest persistence in our prayers. I cannot help but wonder if He pictured Mary when He told this parable.

---

[320] Mark 3:30-34.

[321] John 2:1-5.

[322] Luke 18:1-8.

It is not that He has fallen out of relationship with Mary in either of these two accounts. He is still her son, but He is the head of the family now. He is in charge. He is transitioning into His earthly ministry and leaving behind the responsibilities of the family.

This is why the words from the cross to Mary are so important. There is one more thing to do. As He is dying, He needs to make sure that His mother, who has cared for Him, protected Him in journeys to Bethlehem before He was born, to Egypt to escape a massacre, and back to Nazareth, is also protected. He needs to ensure that she is provided for. He needs to make sure that she is not left destitute and begging on the streets, as some were. He needs to assign her to the loving care of someone He can trust, someone whom she can trust, implicitly. *John.* The disciple with whom He had a close friendship. The one who stood with Mary at the cross.

How often do you think that Jesus has abandoned you? Left during your deepest moment of need. You need to remind yourself – and you know something in hindsight that they did not know at the cross – that Jesus has promised never to leave nor forsake you. He lives and is raised from the dead.

He also entrusts you to the care of another. He does not care for us all on His own. He sends the Holy Spirit. The other Counsellor. The one like Him. You will never be abandoned. Never left. Never forsaken. Whatever life, your feelings or your circumstances tell you, you are not alone! You have a friend who is closer than a brother, closer than a mother or a father too for that matter.[323] One who is so intwined in your life that sometimes His presence is taken for granted or forgotten. He is so close to you right now that He will be reading these words alongside you, prompting your heart to know that it is going to be okay, that the devil doesn't win, that you're a walking miracle of His love and grace, that you matter, that He personally loves you and provides for you. Family matters. He's your Lord. He's also your brother as a joint heir with Him. Why not spend some time thanking Him for being here with you, right now? Make it real again with Him!

---

[323] Proverbs 18:24.

CHAPTER TWENTY-TWO

Alone

"ELI, ELI, LAMA SABACHTHANI?" that is, "MY GOD, MY GOD, WHY HAVE YOU FORSAKEN ME?" [324]

You may have experienced loneliness in your life. At times most people feel lonely. Humanity has a need for company; human beings generally do not exist well in a social vacuum.

McCauley Culkin made his name in the *Home Alone* movies. They tell the story of a young boy's antics when his family leave him alone and how he has to fight off invading burglars. Lots of slapstick comedy follows as the boy pulls off amazing feats of engineering to thwart the bad guys. He has not been forgotten, just left behind. Jesus' aloneness is not the same thing at all.

I mentioned previously that my brother and I knew a time in our lives when there was no parent in the home. This was not the best time and something we kept secret from the authorities and even the church where we attended. Life was different in the 1980s than today but the fact remained that for nearly three years our mother lived with her then boyfriend, visiting us once or twice weekly to ensure there was food in the house or to intervene during the inevitable fights that broke out. The situation came to a crescendo when our home was burgled and, when nothing of much value was found, was set alight by an arsonist. This left my brother and me homeless, so we too moved into the boyfriend's home for a time. This turned into a

---

[324] Matthew 27:46.

few months and was the longest time we had shared a roof with our mother for years. Her boyfriend was a Hindu and struggled having two Bible-believing, exuberant teenagers in the house. Things came to a head and because we were not *technically* homeless, we were going to have to move back into the shell of our home until the authorities would rehouse us.

Unbeknownst to us, our mother had been given a choice; to secure a new home she would have to move with us but her boyfriend's ultimatum was, "Choose me or them, but you cannot have both." This placed her in a real quandary. She loved him. She loved us. She could no longer have it both ways. She was devastated.

I tracked her down to a local park and sat under a tree with her. Conversations like this no teenager should have with their parent. I asked her the question that Jesus asked His Father on the cross: why have you abandoned us? Bless her, she had never seen it this way. I pleaded with her to return. We cried together but I thought that was it. I figured I would end up in foster care. My brother and I moved back to the house. Later there was a knock on the door and I opened it. It was my mother with her belongings. She'd come home.

We were soon rehoused as a family. Whilst that ended that saga there were a few more ups and downs for her in the next year, at the end of which she finally gave her life to Jesus. A happy ending, a new beginning.

My story may be so foreign to you that you cannot relate to it. That's good because no one should relate to this kind of life. Your history may, however, resonate deeply with mine. You may have been through worse, much worse. The abandoned relate to the words of Jesus on the cross, not just in theological sense, but in an experiential way too. Too many people today know what it is like to have a parent deliberately, selfishly and inexplicably decide to walk out on them. It scars the human soul with a wound that is often too deep for counselling and time to heal. It needs the miracle of the One who was abandoned beyond abandonment to intervene.

When Jesus cries out He is reclaiming the fellowship that you can have with the Father. He is making a way for you back to Father God that no one else could make. He is making a way for your healing that no one else can establish, to be loved and lavishly embraced by your true Father. In His suffering there is hope for you in yours. He knows. He knows what it feels like to have the One you loved beyond life itself turn deliberately from you in your greatest hour of need.

God did not do this out of vindictiveness. He did not do this out of selfishness. He did this out of love for you. He is allowing His Son to die, alone, with the full weight and punishment for your sins on His shoulders so that you can become His child too. Jesus did not die out of some masochistic tendency to derive pleasure from pain. He died alone out of love for you.[325] His aloneness was complete, separated from Father's love. The radiance of heaven that had warmed His life now turned cold and sin's black stench crawled over His broken body, claiming Him as its own.

Jesus knows why this is happening. He understands the why in terms of theology, so His "why" from the cross is not a lack of head knowledge. It is the depth of the utter and total isolation that now ravages His heart that brings out this cry. That is why, a few weeks later, Matthew's words that end his Gospel are so poignant:

> *"And surely I am with you always, to the very end of the age."*[326]

Having been left alone, Jesus promises that He will never leave you alone. He was forsaken so that you will never have to be away from God's side of the equation. You may walk off but He is never far. He has a special place in His heart for you. He died for you.

God too promises never to leave you nor forsake you.[327] He has allowed His Son to go through the worst death possible to allow you full access to Him. There is a place in God's heart purchased for you by the blood of His Son Jesus. Even when you wander away from His love, He too, like Jesus, is never far off.[328]

During those tough years when I was alone and abandoned by parents, I was not lonely. It was more than having the company of my brother. I never felt abandoned by God or Jesus or the Holy Spirit. Sure, I asked, "Why?" More than once! It did not seem fair. It did not seem right or normal. But abandoned by God? Never! I understood as a teen-man that Jesus had been alone so that I would

---

[325] John 15:3; Romans 5:8.
[326] Matthew 28:19b.
[327] Hebrews 13:5.
[328] Hosea 14:4 (NKJV).

never have to be. I can now say, with no hint of irony, that I had the best mum in the world. To some she was domineering. To others heartless. To others an epitome of a caring community worker; no one is all bad! To me she was Mum. Not perfect. She did the best she could with the tools in her toolbox. From the perspective of a healed heart, she was priceless.

It's true for you too. Allow God to begin the healing of the burst and broken heart that Jesus has purchased for you on the cross. Allow His sacrifice in this area to mean something for you right now, today. Allow His love – His lavish, unquenchable love – to heal the hurt you have lived with for so long.

CHAPTER TWENTY-THREE

Dying

"I am thirsty."[329]

There is a certain irony, according to one commentator, that the One who quenched all thirst now thirsts.[330] Three things are happening here. Firstly, there is Jesus' physical suffering. Blood loss has led to dehydration. He is dying. Secondly, the Gospel of John tells us that He states this so that Scripture can be fulfilled. It is not a particular Old Testament passage that is being fulfilled though, but rather the testimony of the Gospel writers, who say that Jesus would suffer and die.[331] Thirdly, Jesus is separated from God. He has been sustained throughout His life by the Father; being cut off from that sustenance brings a spiritual thirst too. His humanity is crying out for the presence of God.

How often do you feel dry and thirsty spiritually, even though Jesus promised you that you would never thirst if in communion with Him?[332] When cut off from His presence drying out begins to set in. Jesus, now cut off from Father, experiences the thirst that humanity has: for God. The weight of the sins of the world bear down on Him, separating Him from Father. This is a paradox. Jesus is still fully God, yet He is separated from the tangible presence of the Father and

---

[329] John 19:28.
[330] J. Michaels, John Ramsey, NIBC; Paternoster Press: Carlisle (1995); 328.
[331] ibid.
[332] John 4:13-14.

the Spirit. Sin separates you from God. It is not that God cannot be present where there is sin. He *chooses* not to be, for His pure holiness would condemn you immediately. It is out of His love for us that He withholds His presence at these times, to woo you back to Him and to save you from judgement. He sent Jesus. Jesus dwells with you in your sin. How often do you read in the Gospels that Jesus was hanging out with sinners? He is the friends of sinners. He has already experienced the consequences for the sins you commit. There on the cross, He thirsts.

CHAPTER TWENTY-FOUR

Job Done!

"It is finished!" [333]

It's not how you start; it's how you finish. So the saying goes. There is some truth in that. It is true that a past can be cancelled out by salvation, like pressing the reset button, a new beginning. For those who have had a bad start in life, this can be liberating. For many who are born again, their present situations do not fully reflect the anticipated destination of their beginnings in life.

How you finish is vitally important too. There has to be an aim, an objective, a goal to any task. You have to know when something is finished; sometimes so you can start something new. Things often have seasons in life. Back in the day, it would be expected that people would work for the same employer for their lifetimes, live in the same house all their lives, and even stay with the same bank and utility company. Not so now. Few people stay in one career path for life, and even if they do, they may work for several different employers. Many shop around for the best deals for their households. Sometimes that is wise. The problem is when a church pastor calls for faithfulness, a consistency, to church, a vision, even to the faith, he or she speaks a foreign language. People are not good at finishing things, at seeing something through to its ultimate conclusion. Thank God Jesus did!

---

[333] John 19:30.

It, Not I

"It is finished!" are some of Jesus' best known words. Did you ever wonder why Jesus said *it* and not *I?* He is not talking about Himself. He knows He will continue. He knows He has an eternity of work before Him, interceding for humanity, being present with believers. His body is about to go through the chrysalis of the tomb, but He is not finished. The task is done. The assignment given to Him in Genesis at the Fall – redemption and the claiming back of what was lost in Eden – is complete. It is not His life that has finished. He is not extinguished. Those listening might have thought so.

The Devil's Dilemma

The enemy gleefully rubbed his gnarly hands together salivating at the thought of his cheap victory. Until, that is, he heard the little word 'it'. Panic rose in his devilish heart. Surely Jesus meant, "I..." Surely death had claimed heaven's Champion? A ripple of distant memory swept over his blackened mind as the penny dropped:

> *"...and you will strike his heel."* [334]

Yes, this had now happened. He had tried during Jesus' early years by stirring Herod to kill the young babies of Bethlehem. It took a while to realise he had failed. That early intervention was a failure. Jesus had escaped under the care of His parents. He had tried again in the wilderness. Jesus was exhausted, ripe for the taking, yet frustrated and outwitted by Him, he had left the desert foiled. There had been other tests, other challenges; all had failed.[335] Today though, today had been his greatest triumph. He had orchestrated it brilliantly. Jesus was there on the cross dying.

So why 'it'? The memory continued, the part he had trained his blackened mind to forget:

> *"...he will crush your head..."* [336]

His head began to spin. *It, it, it!* He had been played for a fool. All this time he thought he was conducting events, killing heaven's

---

[334] Genesis 3:15c.
[335] Luke 4:13.
[336] Genesis 3:15b.

Glory, usurping God's plan, creating a fresh vacancy in the Trinity into which he could gleefully stroll, taking his 'rightful' place in heaven as God.

He looked with spiritual eyes to the throne room. God's face was turned away. Angelic beings stood, wings outstretched, ensuring the sight of what was happening at Golgotha could not be seen by Father.

The enemy looks back to Jesus; he sees the dark slime of sin enveloping Him, raining blow upon blow upon Him, the sins of humanity crushing the life out of Him. He feels sick to the stomach as realisation dawns: God planned the whole thing. He has been fooled. His folly complete.

He thought back to Job. How he had wanted to kill the God-fearing Job! He represented everything the devil did not. How his life would have looked good in his trophy cabinet. God had restricted Him. He could do anything but not kill him.[337] Look how that turned out. Job had ended up more prosperous, more in love with God, more devout.

His brain searched the Scriptures. He knew them well, a powerful tool in his manipulative arsenal, to misquote and deceive those who loved God. There it was, laid out before him, the 'it': forty-four Messianic prophecies overwhelmed him. Three stood out, cutting through him like a surgeon's scalpel: Messiah hanging on a cross with criminals; Messiah's atoning death; Messiah's resurrection![338] In that moment, the keys of death and hell jangled around his scaly neck. He knew that he was a pawn. He had conducted nothing. God had willed this from the beginning. He had lost.

He could hear humiliation knocking at the door of his narcissistic dark heart. His failure was being trumpeted before the whole of the heavens. He felt his power leaving him; he was being disarmed, stripped of authority. Instead of ousting heaven, heaven was ousting him. He was losing his power on earth.

---

337 Job 1:12.

338 Psalm 22:16-18; Isaiah 53:2; 5-12; Psalm 24:7-10. There are hundreds of prophecies that Jesus could not have possibly fulfilled by trying to manipulate the situations around Him. For a list of forty-four specific Messianic prophecies that Jesus had no control over, visit: http://christianity.about.com/od/biblefactsandlists/a/Prophecies-Jesus.htm.

No one must ever know, he thought, for if they did they would fear nothing. If he could predict rather than manipulate the future, he would have seen the Apostle Paul writing words that would encapsulate the moment of his defeat and Jesus' triumph:

> *And having disarmed the powers and authorities, he made a public spectacle of them, triumphing over them by the cross.*[339]

Retreating, a scheme developed in his wicked mind: he would make people believe that he had killed Jesus, that some celestial deal had been done to placate him, for if people knew the truth they would follow God wholeheartedly, like Job, like the heroes of faith. His constant, drip-fed lie to weak-minded God-followers that he was equal to God and, therefore, omniscient, all knowing, would be one of his proudest achievements. The truth is, he knew he was not, although he preferred to believe his own publicity. He would deceive them into thinking the price for sin was paid to him, not God. He would inflate his importance in the minds of all who followed Christ. This 'it' of salvation must never gain traction.

Sloping away from Golgotha, he tried to ignore Jesus' next words.

Finished!

John, when later writing his Gospel, picks up on Jesus' words and uses them himself. It's like he wants to emphasise what Jesus is going to say before He says it! He writes:

> *Later, knowing that all was now completed ... Jesus said, "It is finished."*[340]

John is saying, from his perspective beneath the cross, Jesus knew His task was finished, and therefore says so twice for emphasis. For John, this is a double whammy! It is really finished! The word for completed and finished are the same word in the Greek text, *tetelestai,* meaning 'to finish, complete or accomplish'. It is the same word used to speak of Jesus in Hebrews 12:2:

---

[339] Colossians 2:15.
[340] John 19:28a,30b.

> *Let us fix our eyes on Jesus, the author and perfecter of our faith, who for the joy set before him endured the cross, scorning its shame, and sat down at the right hand of the throne of God.*[341]

Other translations used the word 'finisher'. Both 'perfecter' and 'finisher' are trying to describe something that Jesus wants you to know about His atoning sacrifice: *it's done!*

Few Things Are Ever Finished

Life is full of cycles, events that happen again and again; such things are never really finished. They might be finished... until next time.

There are two incredible inventions that are, in my mind, waiting to come out of some science whizz's laboratory. Firstly, a self-cleaning car. I know when I wash and wax my car I can stand back and take some satisfaction in a job well done. It is finished... until next time. The only way to avoid a next time is to park in the garage and never drive it. Even that will not really work. There are plenty of car enthusiasts who rarely drive their pride and joy, keeping it safe from harm in their garage, and still spending an inordinate amount of time cleaning and polishing every part.

The other thing I would love to see is self-cutting grass. I know that artificial grass exists but it is not the same. Each time I mow the lawn I wonder why some boffin has not come up with the idea of grass that will grow to the desired length and no further. When I am done mowing I survey my work but know I shall be back doing this again in a short time.

Much in life is cyclical. Tasks at work are repetitive; finish one, start another. Families live in cycles of recurring patterns: take the kids here today, somewhere else tomorrow, washing today, more tomorrow, cleaning today, more tomorrow... Well, you get the idea! Few things are ever truly finished.

It was the same for the forgiveness of sins under the law and sacrificial system of the Old Testament. Paul observed throughout the book of Romans that the law cannot actually save anyone from their

---

[341] Emphasis mine.

sins – not totally, not completely. In the Old Testament, there was a sacrificial system in place which meant that a person would have to repeatedly come to the priests to sacrifice for their sins. They lived in a cycle of sin, sacrifice, sin, sacrifice.[342] This applied to the nation of Israel too.

When Jesus said, "It is finished," He was abolishing the old system, for the ultimate lamb, the Lamb of God, had been sacrificed. The cycle was broken. Sacrifices are done with for no one can add to Jesus' own sacrifice.

This does not mean that the cycle of sin is broken. You are still human and live in a decaying body. You still face temptations. Sometimes you win, sometimes you fail. What you do not have to do is run down to the local pet store, buy a couple of doves and sacrifice them for your sin. God's wrath and anger against you has been sated. He is no longer angry towards you for He sent Jesus to stand, live and die as you could not: without sinning.

You do, however, have to run to Him when you commit a sin. Sometimes these are committed knowingly, sometimes unknowingly, but when you feel the conviction of the Holy Spirit's witness in your heart, you have to repent. This is not a repentance of salvation. It is a repentance that recognises you are being sanctified. It means you are on a journey, not *to* faith, but *of* faith, where you recognise that God's love for you is boundless. If you want your relationship with Him to be richer and fuller, you will come back to Him, embracing His love again, until Jesus returns or calls you home. This pattern is seen in the early church:

> *This is the message we have heard from him and declare to you: God is light; in him there is no darkness at all. If we claim to have fellowship with him yet walk in the darkness, we lie and do not live by the truth. But if we walk in the light, as he is in the light, we have fellowship with one another, and the blood of Jesus, his Son, purifies us from all sin. If we claim to be without sin, we deceive ourselves and the truth is not in us. If we confess our sins, he is faithful and just and will forgive us our sins and purify us from all unrighteousness. If we claim we have not*

---

342 Leviticus 4-6.

> *sinned, we make him out to be a liar and his word has no place in our lives.*[343]

The Christian life is marked by changed behaviour, the fruit of repentance, and the fruit of the Spirit; change that occurs from the inside out, not the outside in. Cheapening His love and grace by claiming to love Him whilst no change takes place, no lifestyle change or moral change, is to deny the power of salvation. Your internal compass now works to true north: God's will. So you cannot claim to know Him yet walk in darkness.

If we walk in the light we have fellowship with Him and each other.[344]

This means that not all behaviours are acceptable. Sin is not a metaphysical phenomenon for the Christian that is no longer a reality. Sin is still real, although it's not enjoyable anymore. Its consequences are real too. You may be forgiven of something but still have to walk through the consequences of your actions, especially when others have been affected by your sin. You may also lose fellowship with God and with other Christians if you live in darkness, a sinful life, and not in the light.

Does this mean salvation can be lost? When someone says to me salvation can be lost I think of the magnitude of Jesus' sacrifice and the power of His blood. My mind travels to those who are going to enter into heaven by the skin of their teeth, escaping the flames.[345] I ponder Hebrews 6 where it seems to state that salvation can be lost. Essentially, if you're reading this thinking, "Have I lost my salvation?" the answer is no. Those who think they cannot lose their salvation, who can live a raucous life, may be in for a surprise one day when they get to heaven to be turned away.[346] The real issue is that God will ultimately not allow Jesus' sacrifice to be mocked.

Certainly, 1 John says a Christian cannot claim to be without sin. I am a sinner. You are a sinner. That is true. But it is a half-truth. Sinners, yes, but sinners *saved by grace.* The New Testament has a brilliant shorthand way of describing a sinner saved by grace: saint!

---

343 1 John 1:5-10.
344 1 John 1:6.
345 1 Corinthians 3:15.
346 Matthew 7:21-23.

You cannot lie to God and think that the sin you sometimes commit is just a behaviour. It is not. Before you were a Christian you just lived for yourself. You did not know what sin actually was, did not know how it pollutes, but now things are different.

Tetelestai[347] means that sin's punishment is dealt with at the cross. It means you can go back to God and claim the forgiveness that Jesus has died for, time and time again. He does not grow weary of this. He does not tire of lavishing His love on you. He wants you to return to Him. He wants you to *sin less* but knows that until you are made like Christ you will not be *sinless*. The following words of comfort to your struggling soul refresh the heart:

> *If we confess our sins, he is faithful and just and will forgive us our sins and purify us from all unrighteousness.*[348]

Everyone struggles with something. Even Paul lived in the tension between the call he felt and what he did on occasion.[349] Paul recognises the difference, now he is saved, between what he wills to do and the sinful nature. He describes what everyone experiences when walking with God.

When I became a Christian, some sinful behaviours ended right there in my life: swearing, cheating on exams at school, speaking with dead people (yes, you read that right), and so on. Some things though, when I became a Christian, I did not know were sins at all. It was only as the Father, by His Spirit, began to gently nudge me that I understood that certain things were actually dishonouring the relationship I now had with Him. This has been the case now for the many years I have walked with Him. It's as though God is peeling away the layers to reveal more of Himself. There have been times when a certain behaviour has been identified in me by Him, and I respond with something like, "Abba, that was not a problem last week; why is it the case this week? What has changed?" What changes is Christian growth. God has not changed. He is still the

---

347 See page 201.

348 1 John 1:9.

349 Romans 7:14-20.

same.[350] I am being changed. So are you. Gradually. From glory to glory the Bible says.[351]

This process is not salvation. Salvation happens when you accept Jesus; it's immediate. What is happening here is sanctification.[352] God in His graciousness does not strip you down and put you together again immediately, for you could not handle the transformation and, also, you might fall into the error of thinking your new way of life is purely down to your self-will and not the salvation of God. Repeated attempts to earn salvation are over. Jesus did away with them. What is left is a daily renewal and humbling before your loving Father who lavishes forgiveness upon you and continues to work His purposes in and through you. You cannot add to it. You cannot subtract from it. It is a perfected and finished faith.

The Task Becomes the Title

People are often known by their job roles or qualifications. Ask someone who they are and they will often respond with, "I'm Fred and I'm a builder," or "I'm Maria and I'm a secretary." Jobs often give a person a sense of identity and belonging. It is understandable, as for many individuals, they will spend a third of their time at their place of work. It gives them value and sense of worth.

As Christians our identity is deeper than this but even so, Christians will often describe themselves in terms of what they do, rather than who they are: pastor, Sunday school teacher, deacon or elder, youth worker, worshipper, preacher and so on. This is neither right nor wrong; it's just a fact of our culture that people try to describe themselves in terms of what they do because, sociologically speaking, it tells others where they fit in the community. Some, inflated with their own importance, feel this positions them in a lofty place in a hierarchy. I prefer to see it as a jigsaw rather than a hierarchy. A jigsaw is never complete unless all the pieces are in place; its full beauty can never be realised unless each part is facing the right way up, is where it belongs and is in line with others. Furthermore, although there is importance in the pieces that form the edge, in

350 Malachi 3:6.
351 2 Corinthians 3:18.
352 1 Corinthians 6:11.

God's Kingdom He is the edge; He surrounds the Church and defines where every piece belongs.[353] A jigsaw piece cannot elevate itself above others; to function, each piece has to be on the same level, a flat surface. Whilst there may be many splashes of colour and light in one piece compared to another, each piece only truly finds its value when placed in the puzzle by God. Notwithstanding this, people will still describe themselves by their function before their relationship to others; it's simply easier and gives the other pieces the opportunity to understand where they may fit around each other. It's not a perfect analogy, but it does help in understanding how the Kingdom works.

You also find that there is great stock placed upon titles. Those who have been fortunate enough to gain higher education and obtain earned degrees have the right to place letters after their names. Obtaining professional qualifications allows for this too. My wife has more letters after her name than there are actually in it. I too can put letters after my name. It is not a big deal. My earthy qualifications hang in my study at home, a reminder to me of all the hard work and effort they took, but they are also tucked away from public gaze. Now 'degrees' can be purchased off the internet without earning, or learning, to gain them. There was even a news article recently of a university conferring an honorary degree on a dog.[354] Now that's a smart pooch! Some qualifications become titles. Those with Doctorates of Philosophy, or PhD's, along with medical doctors, gain a title as well as a qualification: doctor. The title describes the job they do. Some doctorates do not describe anything at all, to be fair, except the ability of the student to study an obscure subject into greater irrelevance. Some tasks then become a title and some qualifications describe what the person does.

Jesus, on the cross, gains two titles that describe the work He has done when He declared, "It is finished." The writer of Hebrews identifies them:

> *Let us fix our eyes on Jesus, the author and perfecter of our faith.*[355]

---

[353] 1 Corinthians 12:20.

[354] http://www.mnn.com/family/pets/stories/service-dog-receives-honorary-masters-degree.

[355] Hebrews 12:2.

As I write I am reminded that the greatest author who ever walked the face of the earth is Jesus. He wrote the story of salvation. He did this through the Holy Spirit inspiring over forty different writers, over a 1500-year period, to pen the sixty-six books called the Bible. He has told the story. He has made sure that there are signs that point to the truth: Him. He has made sure that there are no plot loopholes, no opportunity for a Hollywood-type rehashed sequel where the darkness wins. When He authored this with His Father, there were no left out chapters, no possibility of a plan B, no final edits that would allow ambiguity to prevail. It is clear for those who choose to look, and it is summed up in His own words, "I am the way and the truth and the life. No one comes to the Father except through me."[356]

Christianity cannot be added to or supercharged to make it more appealing to those outside of the Church. To use a common euphemism, Christianity cannot be 'made more sexy'. It is already perfect; it is already complete. The problem comes when people add to God's masterpiece of salvation by trying to make it more palatable, more dynamic, more acceptable. This happens when attempts are made to make grace more amazing than it already is; or deny the reality that there is one lifetime to accept Jesus as Lord and Saviour by trying to turn Christianity into an insipid universalism; or make the gospel about wealth and happiness. This is not really about adding to the written Scripture but, in effect, *taking away* from Scripture.[357] Any attempt to do either – add or take away – is to ruin the completeness of the gospel. It's already a masterpiece and does not need the intervention of some spiritualised Banksy, the graffiti artist.

Cecilia Gimenez, a faithful parishioner in her 80s, discovered that you cannot improve on an original. A fresco of Jesus in her local church, where she had attended all of her life, had begun to deteriorate due to moisture. According to her, she decided to 'restore' it with the permission of her priest. Although not particularly valuable, it held great sentimental value to the congregation. She set to work, applying brushstroke upon brushstroke, lashings of brown

---

356 John 14:6.
357 Revelation 22:18-19.

hues, until eventually she admitted defeat and called in professional help. It was then all the problems began. She was derided, castigated and criticised. One art critic commented, "The once dignified portrait now resembles a crayon sketch of a very hairy monkey in an ill-fitting tunic."[358] In other words, the beauty had gone. Perhaps in a hundred years' time people will admire her attempts in a new way.

The point is simple: no one makes salvation more perfect by adding their own childish artwork in crayons over the perfect majesty of salvation with vain attempts to make the gospel more than it already is. It is complete and therefore unchangeable. Salvation has come to you. You are saved.

Jesus has done it all. He is the Author. He is the Finisher. Period.

---

[358] http://www.bbc.co.uk/news/world-europe-19349921.

CHAPTER TWENTY-FIVE

Complete Trust

"Dear Lord Jesus, thank you for Mummy, Daddy, my brothers, sisters, Granny and Grandpa. Thank you for the friends I have. Thank you for loving me. Amen." This kind of prayer is said by millions of children around the world each night before they go to sleep. Sometimes the words are repeated after Mum or Dad as they teach their little ones to be thankful and to remember that God loves them.

One of the joys of being a parent is to read to your children at bedtime and teach them how to pray. Recently my wife and I were talking about the prayers we would say at bedtime as we were growing up. I was surprised to learn that she felt that her parents, according to her memory anyway, rarely, if ever, tucked her in at night and prayed with her. Being the youngest of four she was simply part of the crowd. We mused over this for a while and then she asked what kind of prayers I said at bedtime. None. I didn't grow in a Christian home. I was taken to see an Anglican priest at the age of eight or nine by Mum and taught the Lord's prayer by him as a way to fend off evil, but this was hardly a bedtime prayer, although I did say it at bedtime for a while. We then reflected on how we would read to our three sons, the Narnia Chronicles being a favourite as they grew, and pray with them at bedtime. We hoped they each remembered these times and how special they were to us.

Jesus' last words on the cross were:

"Father, into your hands I commit my spirit."[359]

On the face of it, Jesus is quoting Scripture – Psalm 31:5, to be exact. There is the reminder to all those listening that God wins. Jesus' trust, and his knowledge of the Scripture, is complete. God's wrath is being appeased for eternity by the eternal sacrifice of the Son, the atonement in action. The moment in history when sin's power was broken. The last breaths of the Saviour escaping his lips as His heart slows to a halt.

John doesn't say Jesus died or expired. He tells us that at this moment Jesus *gave up* His spirit, His life, for you.[360] He did not have to. Even at that last moment, Jesus could have used His last breath to call the angels to the rescue; He could have saved His own life. He didn't.

Jews had a bedtime prayer that they would teach to their children. They took this very seriously. The prayer was based on this very psalm – Psalm 31 – and was said just before a child would fall asleep; their last words before sleep overwhelmed them.[361] These were the words Jesus spoke aloud!

It must have been a poignant, devastating moment for Mary, for she would have taught Him these words, this very prayer as a toddler. She would have spoken them over God's Son until He was able to recite them Himself. There was also a glimmer of hope in despair too. For these words were not recited merely to have a good night's sleep. Implicit in the rabbinic teaching on the use of this Psalm was that the Lord God would protect one's spirit until they awoke! Jesus' last prayer was one of complete trust: "Watch over me until I wake!" At this moment Jesus was looking forward to the resurrection. The work of salvation, of victory over sin, of taking the punishment, was done. Resurrection would follow. Three days and counting. "Protect my spirit, Father God through my dark times, through my grave, through my wilderness, through my tomb until my resurrection!"

---

[359] Luke 23:46.
[360] John 19:30.
[361] C.A. Evans, *Luke,* NIBC, Hendrickson: Peabody (1990); 344.

Why would God treat you any differently in your darkest moments? The simple and complete trust that Jesus shows on the cross can be yours too during your most desperate times. God promises to take you through the bad stuff, not just avoid it, in life. Christians are brilliant at binding, rebuking and denying any possibility of hardship. Being a Christian, at times, is full of wonder, full of mountaintop experiences, full of joy and laughter. Sometimes it is full of slime and grime, hardship and trouble, vilification and, for some, persecution. Paul, apostle superstar, reminds you that life is full of ups and downs but that he had to learn to be content with much and little. He was hungry at times and materially poor; other times he had plenty. He says he can do all things and, by implication, *go through* all things with the strength that Christ gives.[362]

Christians love Philippians 4:13 but are not so enamoured by Philippians 4:12 that must be there to prove the strength of Jesus working through them. No cross, no crown. No test, no testimony. God does not abandon His precious ones in these tough times. He still walks with you through the valley of the shadow of death.[363] If you want to be more Christlike, trust Him.

---

362 Philippians 4:12-13.

363 Psalm 23:4.

Part Seven

He Lives!

"He is not here, He is risen."

Luke 24:6

Chapter Twenty-Six

Mary, Mary!

She dragged her feet as her grief-swelled heart commanded her legs to move. It had been an awful three days. Her Saviour was gone. Coming to anoint Him, to carry out the ritual to cleanse His body, now 'the Resurrection and the Life' was dead, she was lost.[364] How could this be?

Approaching the tomb, the one so generously given by Joseph of Arimathea, another Christ-follower, her heavy heart stopped beating for a second. Standing with her feet rooted to the spot she could not comprehend the sight. The soldiers placed on guard had gone, the tomb was open, its gaping blackness sweeping over the pain in her heart. She dropped her oils, the accessories that she had brought to complete the embalming ritual that they had been denied on the fateful Friday, turned and ran. Her heart was beating fast now as adrenaline pumped through her veins.

Peter. She had to get to Peter…

Finding him with John she blurts out what she thinks has happened: "They have taken Him!" Her concern is with the last loving task she could perform; she does not know where they have laid Him.

Peter and John run to the tomb. Their hearts are pounding too. Anger rises in Peter; the old man begins to struggle with the new one

---

[364] John 11:25.

that has been created. His Lord has gone, but he is riddled with the guilt of a man who left his best friend in His time of need.

John is younger, faster than Peter, and outruns Him. Full of apprehension he arrives at the tomb and peeks in. He sees the linen cloths used to wrap Jesus' body and goes no farther.

Peter barrels in when he arrives, pushes past the younger disciple, and stands there, frozen to the spot in the empty tomb. He now believes Mary. There is no other explanation in their minds; the Romans must have hidden away the broken body of their Lord. There is not even a place to return to for them to be able to mourn.

Leaving, dejected, they simply go to their homes. It's over.

Mary has returned too. As the men leave she is left standing, weeping. Emotionally spent, she nears the emptiness of the tomb and stoops down to look. It is not empty. There are two men dressed in white.

They were angels although she did not know it at this moment. One was sitting where Jesus' head should have been, the other where His feet should have been, looking at her.

Mary is taken aback, but before she can speak, they say in close unison, "Why are you weeping?"

Have you ever wondered why God sometimes asks you the obvious? There are times in a Christian's life when the facts seem to speak for themselves. During the pain of a season, life can be very difficult. You may think that heaven is distant, that God is uncaring, aloof, far way. When He does speak, it's almost as though He says, "What's up?" Facts do not always speak for themselves; there are always two ways of looking at things: the earthbound way; and from heaven's perspective. Mary, Peter and John had limited information in a finite timeframe. The angels had all of heaven's information from an eternal perspective.

She responds with the same words she gave to Peter and John. "They've taken Him; they've hidden Him; He's gone!"

The only part of her statement that was true was that Jesus was not in the place where they had laid Him. He was not there, but He was not where some Roman soldier had chosen to put Him!

She is disturbed by a noise, a presence behind her; that feeling when you are being watched and you turn to see who is there. In her grief, inconsolable, she does not recognise the person. He asks much the same as the angels. Now she is suspicious. There are no Romans in sight, only these three; maybe *they* have removed Him. Perhaps this is the gardener. Perhaps he has had to move the body to do some unknown task. Perhaps it is a cruel game.

She pleads, "If you moved the body, tell me where and I will tend to the corpse."

One word shines light on her heart. One moment, in the midst of the confusion and pain, breaks through and opens the door to a fresh possibility. It is her name. "Mary!"

She had heard her Lord utter her name so often during His life that it was unmistakable as it bounced off of the rocky walls of the crowded tomb.

It's Jesus! She grabs Him, clinging to Him. "Teacher!"

He explains He is in transition. He's on His way to the Father having conquered Hades. She does not want to let go but He gives her a new mission: go and tell the disciples.

She is now a woman possessed with hope and joy. She must tell others. As they've now returned to their homes she will have to round them up. Her task and Jesus' plan are now one.

How can grief turn to joy in a moment? When Jesus speaks your name in the middle of the trial! It is not over until the King has spoken. There is hope when His voice comforts and challenges. There have been times in life when you may have felt that you're dealing with the hired hand, the gardener, rather than directly with Jesus. Take heart! The facts as they present to you are not the whole truth, they are not laid out logically and if they were, you would still only see part of the picture.

Jesus asked Mary the obvious to see where her faith lay. Would she remember His words about the resurrection? Would she have enough faith left to be able to muster hope within? He did not condemn her. He merely spoke her name. So much power, love and triumph in the whisper of her name. Sometimes you just need to know that in the midst of your tomb He still knows your name. Until He spoke her name she still felt alone, even though she was in the presence of her Lord and Saviour and two angels! Heaven was in the tomb with her. It is the resurrection that brings Christians their totally unreasonable hope in the middle of the worst circumstances in life. *He is alive!*

CHAPTER TWENTY-SEVEN

Historical Facts or Hysterical Wishes?

The resurrection has become the fulcrum of the Christian faith. The problem with this is that if someone truly believes that they can deny the resurrection then they have disproven to themselves the whole of the Christian faith. After all, dead people don't live, right?

Recently I was travelling to a meeting and had to cross the Thames, crossing over the Queen Elizabeth II Bridge, which can be a challenge at the best of times. Listening to the radio, a programme came on about death and a person's hope and musings on their death one day, for now they were in their eightieth year. Most of the woman's thoughts surrounded what archaeologists would make of her bones in a thousand years' time. An atheist, she explained her stance: the resurrection could not be possibly true; if it had really happened it would change everything but for her it was a leap of faith, a leap too great to make. I was saddened by the hopelessness she saw in the ending of her life.

The resurrection of Jesus is not just a biblical story, but historical fact. Bill Bright, one of my heroes, has summarised the reasons for the belief in the resurrection as follows.

Firstly, Christ predicted His resurrection. Even though His followers did not understand what He was telling them at the time, they remembered His words and recorded them.[365]

---

[365] Matthew 16:21.

Secondly, Jesus made numerous appearances to His followers. He comforted the mourners outside His tomb on Sunday morning. On the road to Emmaus, He explained things about Himself from the Old Testament. Later, He ate in their presence and invited them to touch Him. Scripture records that Jesus was seen by more than five hundred at one time. Some may argue that a few people could have agreed to a deception, but how can one explain the collaboration of five hundred people?

Thirdly, the unrelenting faith of the disciples is convincing proof of the Resurrection. Those disciples who were once so afraid that they deserted their Lord now courageously proclaimed this news, risking their lives to preach. Their bold and courageous behaviour does not make sense unless they knew with absolute certainty that Jesus had been raised from the dead.

Next, the growth of the Christian church confirms the Resurrection. Peter's first sermon, which dealt with Christ's resurrection, stirred people to receive Him as their living Saviour.[366] That group of believers has multiplied until now it reaches around the world. Today, there are hundreds of millions of believers.

Finally, the testimony of hundreds of millions of transformed lives through the centuries shows the power of the Resurrection. Many have been delivered from addictions. The destitute and despairing have found hope. Broken marriages have been restored. The most conclusive proof for the resurrection of Jesus Christ is that He is living within believers today in all of His resurrected life and transforming power.

The Resurrection sets Christianity apart. No other religious leader has broken the power of death and conquered sin.[367] These are well known arguments for the Christian who has already accepted by faith the resurrection as fact. They help to bolster belief and act as a reminder of the miraculous nature of the resurrection.

The empty tomb is also supported by the historical reliability of the burial story. New Testament scholars agree that the burial is one

---

[366] Acts 2:41.

[367] Bill Bright; *Why the Resurrection Matters to You: Explaining evidence and meaning of the resurrection;* https://www.cru.org/how-to-know-god/did-jesus-christ-really-rise-from-the-dead.html, accessed 15/02/15.

of the best established facts about Jesus. He died. He was buried. Beyond dispute! One reason for this is because of the inclusion of Joseph of Arimathea as the one who buried Christ. Joseph was a member of the Jewish Sanhedrin. He's well known. Too well known for a fictitious story to be circulating which included him for this not to have been challenged by him, other authorities or his friends if it were untrue. He buried Jesus along with others. The disciples could not have circulated a story about him burying Jesus unless it was true.

Big deal? It really is big news, for the burial account and empty tomb account have grammatical and linguistic ties, indicating that they are one continuous account. Therefore, if the burial account is accurate the empty tomb is likely to be accurate as well. Further, if the burial account is accurate then everyone knew where Jesus was buried.[368] Mary, Peter and John all went to the same tomb. The other Gospels bear this out too. If they were in the wrong place one of them would have noticed! If the tomb had not been empty, it would have been evident to all and the disciples would have been exposed as frauds at worst, or insane at best.

There was a tradition that meant that tombs often acted as shrines for those who were grieving. In our society we tend to lay flowers at significant places – graveyards, sure, but when a public figure dies or there is a tragedy that grabs a community's interest, flowers are laid at the site. It was no different in Jesus' day. In fact, tombs became places where shrines were set up to venerate the dead, especially holy men, rabbis, teachers or hoped-for messiahs. Strikingly, Jesus' tomb was never venerated as a shrine. There were at least fifty such sites in Jesus' day. There was no such shrine for Jesus; His bones were not there.[369]

The empty tomb was discovered by women. Again, this does not seem much of an issue today. However, if someone wanted to start a rumour that was unquestionable then they would go to the most recognised source of the day. The testimony of women in first century culture was seen as worthless. This tells us two things. Firstly, Jesus

---

[368] Matt. Perman, *Historical Evidence for the Resurrection,* http://www.desiringgod.org/articles/historical-evidence-for-the-resurrection, accessed 15/02/16.

[369] ibid.

treated women with utter trust and respect during His lifetime and after His resurrection. He raised their profile in society. Secondly, if a myth, a deliberate lie was to be propagated by some subversive group, then the tale would begin with the male disciples discovering the empty tomb, seeing Jesus first. The fact that women were the first witnesses to the empty tomb can only be explained if they were indeed the first to witness this. It is implausible otherwise. It is recorded this way in the Gospels and that quirky fact gives historical credence to the resurrection account.[370]

[370] ibid.

CHAPTER TWENTY-EIGHT

Impossible or Probable?

To use the often quoted Sherlock Holmes' character of Sir Arthur Conan Doyle, "When you have eliminated the impossible, whatever remains, however improbable, must be the truth!" There is enough historical evidence to show that the resurrection is not simply a legend made up by a few supporters of Jesus. It leaves every person with the realisation that they have to take a step of faith. It is not a step into the unknown, nor, in fact, is it a giant leap of faith. It is a simple, logical, next step towards faith. For the dear lady on the radio contemplating her own mortality, she had not heard the evidence that her soul so desired to find; it was as though she wanted to believe but could not.

Five Things the Resurrection Gives You

The resurrection proves the virgin birth and the death of Jesus. The three are intertwined within the Scriptures. If Jesus did not rise from the dead then the virgin birth is a myth. If Jesus is not virgin born, there is no possibility of His resurrection, for why would God validate an imposter? If Jesus did not die, He would not have been fully human, therefore the resurrection would not have occurred. The resurrection is one leg of a very important three-legged stool that faith is rested upon.

The fact of the resurrection of Jesus gives you five things that those who deny its authenticity cannot enjoy.

GIVES HOPE:

The resurrection gives hope for the future. Hope in this context is not just wishful thinking, but in the biblical context, hope becomes a sure fire thing:

> *Now faith is the substance of things hoped for, the evidence of things not seen.*[371]

Hope has substance, is tangible, is weighty. Jesus promises that He is the resurrection and the life. His resurrection promises that you will be raised one day too because He is the resurrection.[372] He proves this by being raised. It is the basis for faith.

BUILDS TRUST:

The resurrection shows that you can trust Jesus implicitly. The resurrection proves all He said to be true. If He were not raised everything He said would be brought into fresh focus on the backdrop of doubt. All the authorities had to do was to produce the body of Jesus to quell any preaching about Christ after He had died. They could not. If the disciples had managed to overpower the Romans on guard duty at the tomb, which would have been more humiliating than anything for them, and hide Jesus' body this would have come to light sooner or later. There were not many places a body could be hidden before being noticed. Decay in a first century setting would set in pretty quickly and be discovered. Even after a few days with a proper burial, Lazarus stank, apparently.[373] Jesus' body could not have been easily hidden or disposed of.

He is risen! This means everything He said is trustworthy. Every promise, every healing, every miracle is true too. It means every promise He speaks over your life today can also be taken at face value. He will not leave you, not abandon you; He will fight your corner, intercede for you, and love you beyond reason.

---

[371] Hebrews 11:1 (NKJV).

[372] John 11:25; Hebrews 11:35; Revelation 20:5.

[373] John 11:39.

CREATES A NEW MINDSET:

Thirdly, because He is risen, you treat death differently than you did before you were a Christian. Think about it a bit. No one likes the idea of dying physically, the mechanics of what takes place, the lack of life. Everyone wants to die peacefully at home in bed, with no illness or disease clawing away their life. No one wants to die in tragic circumstances. This is true even for the Christian. I have some bad news for you: being a Christian is no guarantee of a peaceful death. Some of the most stunning servants of God died in unpleasant ways. Many Christians are being martyred for their faith, even today in the twenty-first century. David Wilkerson, who founded Teen Challenge, who followed God throughout his life, who moved across America to work with gangs in New York, died in an horrendous car crash. It needs to be remembered that the manner in which a Christian dies is not the reward; it is what comes after death that is the reward. The resurrection proves death is defeated, the final enemy vanquished.

The Bible puts it like this:

> *Where, O death, is your victory? Where, O death, is your sting?*[374]

It does not matter how death tries to claim you; awaiting at the end of this is Jesus, keys of death around His neck, smiling to embrace you! The resurrection means death for you is not the end, but the beginning of the rest of a blessed eternity.

This new attitude to death was brought home to my wife and I when she was involved in an accident and dislocated her shoulder. Not life-threatening in itself but my youngest son and I were watching from the corner of the emergency room as they used a drug to knock her out whilst they manipulated the dislocated shoulder back into place. After a minute or so I noticed she was not breathing; the machines were set on silent but were blinking and flashing. I said, "Has anyone checked her breathing? Look at the monitor!" The three medics attending her looked around and immediately began to resuscitate her. They managed to get her breathing so carried on with the procedure. The same thing happened a second time but this time

---

[374] 1 Corinthians 15:55.

they were primed and so acted without my prodding! It took a while longer to get her breathing and they used various techniques to do so. All the while, Sam and I were watching this unfold. At no time did I panic that she was going to die. I was at peace – because I knew that she was not going to leave us yet.

My son was at peace too. I asked him afterwards what he made of all this; I was worried the situation would have upset him. Whilst he admitted it was not easy he remembered a sermon where I had said that God had given me a promise that Barbie and I would live to an old age together, that there'd be no divorce and that we'd grow old together. He said he remembered this in the emergency room and just thought everything would be okay. Then he quipped, "But you *are* old now, right, Dad?" Humour in the midst of difficulty is a trait in our family!

As Barbie was recovering she said to me, "I died!"

I answered, "Almost. Not quite. Why do you say that?"

She then recounted leaving her body, moving into the warmest yellow light and being totally at peace, pain free. Knowing she was dying, she said there was an inevitability about it; peace flowed through her and she did not even look back, but forward to what awaited. She knew she was going to Jesus! She was then pulled back to her body, twice. Next thing, she woke with me holding her good hand, talking to her. It was hard for me to hear that she did not want to look back at Sam and me – my ego was maybe a little dented – but I also understood that she was going to gain more than she was leaving behind.

PROVES JESUS' PROMISES:

Next, the resurrection proves He is coming back. If everything He says is trustworthy then, be assured, He's coming back for you too. John 14:1-4 records Jesus amazing words about this to believers:

> *"Do not let your hearts be troubled. You believe in God; believe also in me. My Father's house has many rooms; if that were not so, would I have told you that I am going there to prepare a place for you? <u>And if I go and prepare a place for you, I will come back and take you to be with me</u>*

> *that you also may be where I am. You know the way to the place where I am going."*[375]

It is so important to understand that Jesus saw His death and resurrection as part of the process of going and preparing a place in preparation for His co-heirs. Why prepare a place if there are to be no occupants of the mansions in heaven? When things are ready, He'll be back for you. The resurrection proves the Second Coming is a reality for the saints!

CHANGES THE PRESENT:

Finally, although this list is in no way exhaustive, the resurrection changes everything for you in life now. Not only is there the sense of optimism, hope and surety of our future in God, there is another promise that is only possible because of His resurrection. He sends the Holy Spirit! Listen to His words again from John's Gospel and the book of Acts:

> *"And I will ask the Father, and he will give you another advocate to help you and be with you forever – the Spirit of truth ... All this I have spoken while still with you. But the Advocate, the Holy Spirit, whom the Father will send in my name, will teach you all things and will remind you of everything I have said to you. He sends the Spirit..."*[376]

> *"...you will receive power when the Holy Spirit comes on you; and you will be my witnesses in Jerusalem, and in all Judea and Samaria, and to the ends of the earth."*[377]

These incredible promises are given by Jesus anticipating the resurrection! He sends the Spirit. The Spirit is only sent and present with you because Jesus has risen and has now taken up His rightful place at the right hand of the Father.[378] This means that the Christian life is a life that has a Counsellor, a guide, a confidant, an empowerer who resides within. This is only possible because of the resurrection! Yet so many miss the opportunity to invite the Spirit to be those

375 Emphasis mine.
376 John 14:16-17,25-26.
377 Acts 1:8-9.
378 Romans 8:34.

things; they are happy with Him being the seal of ownership, happy for Him to identify them as children of God, but do not embrace Him as the power of the new, full life that Jesus promised.[379] The Holy Spirit means the Christian life is powerfully lived now. Ask God to fill you afresh with His Spirit, to give you new gifts of the Spirit, to grow the fruit of the Spirit within you, to transform you. Live that life now, because Jesus died and is risen!

---

[379] 2 Corinthians 1:22; Romans 8:15; John 10:10.

Part Eight

He is Coming Soon

"Look, I am coming soon! My reward is with me, and I will give to each person according to what they have done."

Revelation 22:12

Chapter Twenty-Nine

Not Long Now

He's coming back. He will take those who love Him and, as you read through the last chapters of the Bible, you discover that there will be a renewal of creation where Jesus' new royal priesthood are going to rule and reign.

How will you know Jesus has returned?

In Jesus' humanity there were certain things that were kept from Him, things that give hope to those who are God-followers now, for Jesus had to trust Father implicitly too. One of the most divinely exquisite paradoxes is that Jesus is fully God, but in His humanity some of His divine attributes were shed. God is omniscient; He knows everything. Jesus did not. He is clear about this, and the details of His second advent was an area that is clearly reserved to the Father's knowledge.[380] Jesus went on to describe what the world would look and feel like at that future time, but He did not know exactly when this would be, the day, the hour. Many cults have come and gone that proclaimed they knew the exact time and date of His return; even those masquerading as Christians have claimed a monopoly on knowing what Jesus did not know. The Jehovah's Witnesses have claimed to know the date of His return, erroneously, on many occasions.

Apparently, today Jesus is an Australian who lives in Queensland and claims to have memories of the cross, that the crucifixion was not

---

[380] Matthew 24:36.

too painful and that he is one with God. Before this revelation came to him, he was an I.T. specialist.[381] Good news, then – not only can he fix your soul, but your computer too when it is on the fritz! Over the years many have claimed to be Jesus, reincarnated, invisibly returned, hidden from sight; at least thirty-six people over the last two hundred years or so have made this claim.[382] They cannot all be Jesus, but can one of the them actually be right? Jesus warned us about this trend of cults, religious leaders, copycats and sometimes mentally ill people. All of them have one thing in common according to Jesus: deception. They are deceived and those who try to follow them are too. They are not divine, but sadly deluded.

The Bible is clear about the second coming. There are three hundred and fifty Bible references to the first coming of Christ but two thousand five hundred references to His second coming! If the Bible says it once it will happen, but two thousand five hundred times is not something that can be ignored.[383] There can be no biblical doubt, Jesus will return. His return will have several key features that will mean it will be unmistakable. There will be no ambiguity, no trips to the local mental health unit for Him; you will know it is Him.

---

381 http://news.sky.com/story/1096687/former-it-specialist-claims-to-be-jesus-reborn.

382 https://en.m.wikipedia.org/wiki/List_of_people_claimed_to_be_Jesus.

383 Sermon: Philip Hannam, 11/15, delivered at Life Church Chelmsford.

Chapter Thirty

No Doubt about His Identity

I have friends whom I have not seen for a long time. Social networking has made it possible to follow their lives, at least the bits of their lives they put online, and see the physical changes that age brings. I have other friends whom I have not seen in years and who are not on social networks. When I do occasionally meet them, I still know it is them, for there are certain physical markers that do not change about their face: the distance of their eyes, the shape of their nose, the height of their cheekbones and so on. Imprinted in my brain is the most amazing facial recognition software that tells me this is my friend. At the very least I get an idea that I have seen this person before. In fact, I am better with faces than names. I generally know if I have met someone before. Context helps this too. If I am used to seeing someone in a certain place, church or a business, I will generally associate them with that place. I expect to see them there; my visual sense anticipates their presence. When that fails, and it rarely does, there is another sense that kicks in: hearing.

People's voices rarely change; they may mature with age, they may change pitch slightly, but the recognition software in the recesses of my grey matter still tell me that this is my friend; I recognise their voice even if I have not heard it for a long time. Sometimes I might think I have seen a doppleganger, but their voice betrays them.

I was recently mistaken for someone else in a coffee shop. Two guys thought I was an ex-work colleague. I could see them looking at me and gesturing. In the end they plucked up the courage to ask me if

I was indeed their friend from years ago. As soon as I opened my mouth they knew I was not; I did not have the regional accent their friend did, and my voice was the wrong pitch. As surprising as it is that there are two such incredibly good-looking men on the planet, I accepted their apologies for interrupting my lunch and they made their way out. If I have not seen someone for years my brain still knows their voice.

Jesus will return personally and you'll personally know that it is Him. 1 Thessalonians 4:13-18 reassures you about this. The Lord Himself will appear; personally Him. No mistake will be made over His identity. Humanity will know it is Him; you will just know!

He will appear in the place where you'd expect to see Him, descending from the heavens. Your visual recognition software will know this is where you'd expect to see the returning Messiah, not living in an Australian suburb, but coming through the clouds. A place where no other man could appear from. It will be Jesus! His loud command will tell you it is Him. Jesus noted that His sheep know His voice.[384] His voice will be familiar; it will have authority and command and compassion and hope and joy and triumph.

You will know it is Him. So will the whole world!

He'll Have Scars

Jesus will not return invisibly or in some metaphysical random dimension where he is partially known but remains unseen. He will occupy physical space and time. He will be touchable, tangible, there. He will be present. So will the scars; marks of death that promise life and redemption. His wrists, feet, side, brow and even His back will have those marks that speak of a crown, flogging and crucifixion. He will not be some reincarnated madman with supposed memories of a past life. It will be Him. The gospel has always been incarnational, about the physical nature of Jesus, about God being present. His virgin birth was physical, His resurrection was physical and His second coming will be physical too.[385]

---

384 John 10:27.

385 John 1:14; Luke 24:34-40; Acts 1:11; Sermon: Philip Hannam, 11/15, delivered at Life Church Chelmsford.

Everyone Will See Him

His return will be highly visible. My wife likes a TV program that focuses on the lives of people left behind after a cataclysmic whole world event, but no one seems to understand exactly what has happened. The Bible is not so ambiguous about the ultimate return of Jesus. It is possible the rapture, a subject for another time, may leave some confused because there will be a suddenness to it.[386] Opinion in the Christian community is divided as to what this will actually look like. When Jesus returns to rule and reign though, there will be no mistaking what is happening.[387]

Today is a technological age where most of the world is connected via the Internet, news is instant, and satellites have enabled world events to be viewed everywhere. This spread of technology is creeping thoughout the world, even to parts of the planet that have no television. I have been on ministry trips to some pretty inaccessible places and have seen people begging for water and food in the most arid of climates, yet they still have a mobile phone. People are increasingly connected. Will this be how Jesus is seen by the whole world at once? I do not know. I know God uses technology. I know that, for instance, the timing of Jesus' birth and the spread of the fledgling Church came after the Roman Empire had developed a convenient road and transportation system throughout the known world. I also know that it is within God's power to instantly make everyone aware that Jesus is back without any need for technological help. The Bible says He will be revealed to everyone. No mistakes. No doubt. No news censorship. It will be known it is Him!

Visual Impact!

One of the great traditions around the world on New Year's Eve is to see which country puts on the biggest and the best firework display as the New Year in their time zone is celebrated. It's a sign of the country's wealth, security and prowess. People flock to the events or watch them on their televisions at home, or at least see them on the news the following day having gone to bed early!

---

[386] 1 Thessalonians 4:13-18; 1 Corinthians 15:50-54.
[387] 2 Thessalonians 1:7.

Jesus' first coming was not that public. There were a few shepherds, a group of wise men, and presumably an innkeeper, although he is not actually mentioned in the Gospel text. Whilst angels did appear to the shepherds, and there was a star that was followed by astronomers, not many noticed. When Jesus was born He was vulnerable. His life needed the protection of Joseph and Mary and the intervention of angelic messengers. Heaven's Glory in a feeding trough. Easily extinguishable.

His second coming will be glorious, powerful, invincible, unmistakable. He will appear with angels who will be blowing trumpets and lightning across the skies. As anonymous as His first coming was, so His second coming will be glorious and intentionally unambiguous, outstripping any fireworks display ever devised. It will be loud, sure and attention-grabbing.[388] The victorious King will not enter sombrely on to the stage but with the spoils of victory. Heaven is holding its breath for that moment. Angels know, and you know too, that moment is ever coming closer. Those in the throne room turn their eyes to the Father, waiting for the signal to go! Jesus, too, looks to the Father, awaiting the nod, the command, to go. No false starts. No second attempts. It's soon.

Be Ready

Over the years the second coming of Jesus has been vilified and joked about. People would say, "Look busy, Jesus is coming!" Some would say more vitriolic things. People scoff at the idea of the Victor's return.[389] He's still coming though! Be ready. Jesus instructed His disciples primarily to do two things concerning His return. (These are not the only two things a Christian should do, of course.) Watch. Pray.[390]

Times are accelerating fast. Available knowledge – by that I mean the things anyone can access on the Internet – is increasing exponentially. Scientific discoveries abound as, I believe, God enables human curiosity; wars are increasing; and end time prophecies are being fulfilled all around the world. Moral decline is celebrated as

---

[388] 2 Thessalonians 1:7; Titus 2:11,13.
[389] 2 Peter 3:3-4.
[390] Luke 21:36.

civilised, yet abortion, euthanasia and a lack of care for the poorest and most vulnerable can never be called civilised. Tolerance is the new byword for 'anything goes', until it comes to the Christian Church, whose voice is seen as intolerant for it disagrees with the crowd at large.

You don't need me to tell you things are sliding in society. To watch is to do more than merely observe. It is not to judge; not in the space-grace time. It is to lovingly offer hope in a decaying world. For as you watch the lives of those around you, make no mistake, they are watching yours too. Watching also has to do with keeping guard over your life. Father God calls you holy, a called-out one, one who is separated for His purposes.[391] This means that His people, including you and I, are to reflect who He is to the world, not reflect the world to Him. The Church is His bride but at times it appears engaged to the culture around it. The Church is to be different, culturally and in terms of its values and behaviours. Behaving the same as those who do not know Jesus may appear to be superficially cool, but ultimately the test of the Christian faith is how different a believer is to their peers. That does not mean there is a scale of weirdness, that the more of an oddball a person appears to be, the more Christian they are. True Christians will love those who are lost for they were once lost themselves, but once found, they will change and behave differently for the sin that once offended only God now is offensive to them. That offence is an offence with the self.

Berating and judging the lost for behaving like the lost is not loving. When a Christian sins and the Holy Spirit brings loving conviction to their soul, the Christian bows the knee in repentance again. They know that they are not perfect but are on a journey towards perfection which will be truly fulfilled one day in Christ's presence.[392]

Jesus told His followers to pray. Given the moral slide in society, the Church is often inclined only to pray, "Come, Lord Jesus!" It's a biblical prayer,[393] but it can be said in an unbiblical way. Praying for the Lord's return should be to usher Him in as the victorious King.

---

[391] 1 Peter 1:16.
[392] 1 Corinthians 15:52-53.
[393] Revelation 22:20.

Praying He returns to rescue a feeble bunch of Christians, standing at a spiritual bus stop in the rain awaiting rescue from the world, is not really what Jesus had in mind. Pray for the Lord's return, but pray He comes in victory when all His purposes and plans are complete on the earth, not because you feel uncomfortable in your current circumstances. To pray in this context is to intercede for the world. It is to ask for the same grace that you have been shown to be shown to the drunken man on the street, the young prostitute who cannot make ends meet, the drug addict who is so full of heroin that life is slipping away, the married couple next door who argue every night keeping you awake.

To pray is to stand in a gap where they cannot stand themselves and plead with God as Abraham did for Sodom and Gomorra.[394] He starts pleading with God and chooses the random number of fifty; if there are fifty people who are righteous, will God spare the place? Yes, God will. He is gracious. Abraham thinks about this for a moment and realises that there probably are not fifty people worth saving there and so one of the most interesting negotiations takes place in the Bible. It's like a reverse auction. Eventually Abraham settles on ten people; if there are ten righteous people in the whole city, will God spare them? Yes, God will. He's slow to anger and swift to bless; it's in His nature.[395] There were not even ten: just Lot, his wife and two daughters made it to the city limits, and then his wife looked back and turned to salt, so only three made it to safety.[396] All that prayer, intercession and pleading for just three in the city to be ushered to safety.

How many are there in your community, your city, your province that need salvation? Pray for them all; plead for their souls. Perhaps all will come through, perhaps revival will break out, perhaps a spiritual revolution will take place. Or maybe just a handful will make it into the Kingdom. One thing I know: if the Church does not pray, none get saved; when the Church prays, many do.

---

[394] Genesis 18:16-33.

[395] Exodus 34:6.

[396] Genesis 19.

Epilogue: Over to You!

The most important question anyone will ever answer will be put to them by Father God. One day, a fateful and great day, He will ask everyone individually what they did with His Son. The answer to that question will determine a person's individual destiny. My hope and prayer is that journeying through these pages has helped show the immeasurably great weight of His love towards you. I pray you have had your love renewed and warmed for Jesus once more. If you are a Christian you may be wondering why I did not choose some obvious verses to look at, perhaps some of your personal favourites that I seem to have deliberately overlooked. Any book about Jesus is going to be incomplete. The Christian faith is a paradox, for you know the unknowable, and describe daily the indescribable. He is beyond mere words to adequately picture Him, yet you know Him intimately. He is truly exquisite. Take the advice in these pages. Walk closer to Him. He will not fail you.

Perhaps you are not yet a born again believer. You have read this book with some degree of curiosity, but with a sense of growing wonder. Maybe the sacrifice that Jesus has made for you has made sense for the first time. If that's you, and you would like to accept Jesus as your Lord and Saviour, then say the following prayer:

> *Jesus, thank you for coming and dying in my place. Thank you for taking the punishment that was mine. Thank you for taking God's anger so that I can receive His love. Forgive me of my sins, wrongdoings, and come and live in my heart. Fill me with your Holy Spirit and make me the person you want me to be. In Jesus' name, Amen!*

That's it. It is that simple to begin a new life in Father God, full of wonder, joy and possibilities. Tell someone what you have done, a friend you know is a Christian. They will help you find a church near you, help you get started reading God's love letter to you, the Bible, and answer questions you are bound to have. Welcome to the family!

Additional Notes

i. J. Michaels, John Ramsey, NIBC; Paternoster Press: Carlisle (1995); 88.
The reason for the waters being "stirred" has never been satisfactorily answered but was probably due to the movement caused by the presence of an intermittent spring. These waters may have been rich in minerals and may have been warm. Later insertions in the text claiming an angel stirred the waters and the fact that the first one into the waters would be cured seem to be there to explain the man's statement about needing help. The NIV rightly puts these in the margin rather than the main text. Clearly this was not the work of an angel. Archaeological evidence has shown that the Romans frequented this pool too for its medicinal benefit and attributed the water's healing properties to the pagan god Asclepius. Certainly in Jesus' time the practice of bathing here for healing was frowned upon by orthodox Jews not least as it was frequented by Jews and pagans alike.

ii. http://www.biblestudytools.com/dictionary/bethesda, accessed 15/07/15.
Bethesda: house of mercy, a reservoir (Gr. kolumbethra, "a swimming bath") with five porches, close to the sheep-gate or market (Nehemiah 3:1; John 5:2). Eusebius the historian (A.D. 330) calls it "the sheep-pool". It is also called "Bethsaida" and "Beth-zatha" (John 5:2, RSV marg.). Under these "porches" or colonnades were usually a large number of infirm people waiting for the "troubling of the water". It is usually identified with the modern so-called Fountain of the Virgin, in the valley of the Kidron, and not far from the Pool of Siloam (q.v.); and also with the Birket Israel, a pool near the mouth of the valley which runs into the Kidron south of "St. Stephen's Gate." Others again identify it with the twin pools called the "Souterrains", under the convent of the Sisters of Zion, situated in what must have been the rock-hewn ditch between Bezetha and the fortress of Antonia. But quite recently Schick has discovered a large tank, situated about one hundred feet north-west of St. Anne's Church, which is, as he contends, very probably the Pool of Bethesda. No certainty as to its identification, however, has as yet been arrived at.

iii. http://www.bibleistrue.com/qna/qna22.htm, accessed 30/04/15.
It's important to note that betrothal was of a much more formal and far more binding nature than the 'engagement' is with our culture. Indeed, it was held to be a part of the transaction of marriage, and as being the most binding part. The ceremony of betrothal consisted in the acceptance before witnesses of the terms of the marriage as contracted for. God's blessing is then solemnly asked on the union now provided for, which will probably take place only after some months, or perhaps even some years. No further financial negotiations were allowed after the betrothal is placed into effect. This engagement was considered so binding that if for any reason the marriage could not take place, the woman could not marry another unless a proper procedure was followed and a paper of divorce was written. While the marriage may have been intended by the parents from the infancy of both parties, the formality of betrothal is not entered into until the marriage is considered reasonably certain. A prolonged interval between betrothal and marriage was considered undesirable on many accounts, though often an interval was needed for the groom to render the agreed upon service or to pay the price. Even in these situations the time interval was usually no more than a year or two (though in the case of Jacob, it was seven years!). Again, the betrothed couple were legally in the position of a married couple, and any unfaithfulness was 'adultery' (Deuteronomy 22:23; Matthew 1:19).
For more on this see *Marriage and Betrothal in Bible Times* on the same site.

iv. W. Jackson; Caiaphas – *Official at the Trial of Jesus;* https://www.christiancourier.com/articles/664-caiaphas-official-at-the-trial-of-jesus, accessed 19/08/15.
In 1990, just south of Jerusalem, a Jewish burial cave was accidentally discovered. When the cave was finally entered, archaeologists found several limestone ossuaries (boxes containing bones). One of these contained the remnants of several persons, including those of a man about sixty years of age. The box was elaborately decorated, suggesting that it housed the remains of someone important. On the exterior were these words, 'Joseph, son of Caiaphas,' or, as scholars suggest the meaning may be, 'Joseph of the family of Caiaphas.' 'Caiaphas' was apparently a family nickname. According to Josephus, the High Priest who succeeded Annas was 'Joseph Caiaphas.' Ronny Reich, of the Israel Antiquities Authority, suggests that these bones are 'in all probability' the bones of that same High Priest who prosecuted Jesus Christ.

v.http://www.myjewishlearning.com/article/history-ofbar-mitzvah/, accessed 30/12/15.
Schauss traces bar mitzvah from biblical and talmudic times, when it meant simply reaching the age of majority, through later ceremonial observances of the occasion. Particularly interesting is his focus on customs surrounding the bar mitzvah ceremony, both in Ashkenazic and Sephardic traditions. He also suggests why it became traditional for the bar mitzvah to read the maftir, the last of the section of the Torah portion on a Shabbat. Adapted with permission from The Lifetime of a Jew Throughout the Ages of Jewish History (UAHC Press, now out of print). In the Bible, a man reached the age of majority at age twenty, when he was eligible for war and taxation. In talmudic times, the age of majority was moved to thirteen, and in recognition of the son's change in status, the father pronounced a blessing in which he praised God for relieving him of responsibility for his son's conduct. But no celebration marked the occasion.

Contact the Author

To contact the author, please write to:

Life Church
Hall Street
Chelmsford
Essex
CM2 0HG
United Kingdom

Or send an email to:

exquisitejesus@hotmail.com